S·H·P
THE
SCHOOLS
HISTORY
PROJECT

DISCOVERING THE PAST

DISCOVERING THE
ROMAN EMPIRE

Colin Shephard (Director, SHP)
Mike Corbishley

Scott
O'Hagan

JOHN MURRAY

Acknowledgements

Illustrations by David Anstey; Peter Bull Art Studio; Art Construction; John Lupton/Linden Artists; Chris Rothero/Linden Artists.

Further illustrations reproduced by kind permission of: **p.2** *bottom* Editions Albert René/Goscinny–Uderzo; **p.21** from *The Roman World* by Mike Corbishley, Kingfisher Books, © Grisewood and Dempsey Ltd, 1986 **p.49** from *Energy through Time* by Joe Scott, Oxford University Press.

Photographs reproduced by kind permission of:
cover: Trustees of the British Museum; **p.1** Trustees of the British Museum; **p.2** *top left* C.M. Dixon; *top right* Grosvenor Museum, Chester; **p.3** *top left* Ronald Sheridan/Ancient Art and Architecture Collection; *top right* Rheinisches Landesmuseum, Trier; *centre* Musée du Louvre, Paris/Réunion des Musées Nationaux; *bottom left and right* Mary Evans Picture Library; **pp.4/5** C.M. Dixon; **p.6** Mansell Collection/Alinari; **p.8** *top* The Mansell Collection; *bottom* Peter Clayton; **p.13** Mary Evans Picture Library; **p.16** Ronald Sheridan/Ancient Art and Architecture Collection; **p.17** *top left* Werner Forman Archive; *top right* G.T. Garvey/Ancient Art and Architecture Collection; *bottom right* Mansell Collection/Alinari;

p.18 Alan Sorrell © Mark Sorrell (photo: F.W. Wombwell–Robinson); **p.19** Ronald Sheridan/Ancient Art and Architecture Collection; **p.20** C.M. Dixon; **p.23** The Hulton Deutsch Collection; **p.24** *top* Ronald Sheridan/Ancient Art and Architecture Collection; *botttom* C.M. Dixon; **p.25** *top* Musée du Louvre, Paris/Réunion des Musées Nationaux; *centre left and right* Trustees of the British Museum; **p.26** The Museum of London; **p.27** *top, centre bottom, bottom left* Mansell Collection/Alinari; *centre top, bottom right* C.M. Dixon; **p.29** *top, bottom* C.M. Dixon; *centre* Sonia Halliday Photographs; **p.31** Peter Clayton; **p.32** *centre* C.M. Dixon; *bottom left* Rheinisches Landesmuseum, Trier; *bottom right* Dr P.J. Reynolds/Butser Ancient Farm; **p.35** *top* Alan Sorrell/English Heritage; *bottom* English Heritage; **p.36** Mansell Collection/Alinari; **p.37** Grosvenor Museum, Chester; **p.39** Ronald Sheridan/Ancient Art and Architecture Collection; **p.41** Ivan Lapper/English Heritage **p.43** English Heritage; **p.45** English Heritage; **p.46** *top* Ronald Sheridan/Ancient Art and Architecture Collection; *bottom* Michael Holford; **p.49** C.M. Dixon; **p.50** *left* Mary Evans Picture Library; *centre* Peter Connolly; **p.52** C.M. Dixon; **p.53** Mary Evans Picture Library; **p.55** Sonia Halliday and Laura Lushington **pp.56/7** Roger Wood; **p.59** Jason Wood; **p.61** Trustees of the British Museum.

THE SCHOOLS HISTORY PROJECT

This project was set up by the Schools Council in 1972. Its main aim was to suggest suitable objectives for History teachers, and to promote the use of appropriate materials and teaching methods for their realisation. This involved a reconsideration of the nature of History and its relevance in secondary schools, the design of a syllabus framework which shows the uses of History in the education of adolescents, and the setting up of appropriate examinations.

Since 1978 the project has been based at Trinity and All Saints' College, Leeds, where it is one of three curriculum development projects run and supported by the Centre for History Education. The project is now self funding and with the advent of the National Curriculum it has expanded its publications to provide courses throughout the Key Stages for pupils aged 5–16. The project provides INSET for all aspects of National Curriculum History.

ontents

N.B. Words in SMALL CAPITALS are defined in the glossary on page 63.

Who were the Romans?

1. What is your image of the Romans? Write down three words that sum up the Romans for you.

SOURCES 1–8 show various pictures of Roman people and of things that the Romans made. In this unit we will be using evidence like this to investigate life in the Roman EMPIRE, 2000 years ago. You'll need to look carefully at the evidence.

2. Look at Sources 1–8. Which ones best fit your ideas about the Romans?
3. Decide which of Sources 1–8 were made at the time of the Roman Empire – from the first to the fourth centuries AD.
4. Which of the sources were made more recently – in the last 150 years?
5. What do these sources tell us about the Romans – for example, how they dressed and what they did in their leisure time?
6. What else would you like to find out about the Romans?

▲ **SOURCE 1** The painting on the cover of a Roman man's coffin. He was buried in Egypt in the third century AD

▲ **SOURCE 2** A modern reconstruction of what a Roman soldier would have looked like in the first century AD, and the weapons he would have carried

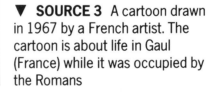

▼ **SOURCE 3** A cartoon drawn in 1967 by a French artist. The cartoon is about life in Gaul (France) while it was occupied by the Romans

© 1992 LES ÉDITIONS ALBERT RENÉ/GOSCINNY-UDERZO

▲ **SOURCE 4** An aqueduct in Spain, built by the Romans in the second century AD to carry fresh water for the city of Segovia

▲ **SOURCE 5** A wall painting from the third century AD showing farmworkers in Roman-occupied Germany

▲ **SOURCE 6** A carving from the second century AD showing four stages in a boy's life

▲ **SOURCE 7** A picture of Roman women, painted about 100 years ago

▲ **SOURCE 8** A drawing of gladiators, who fought to the death to entertain Roman people. It was drawn about 100 years ago

From village to Empire

The beginnings of Rome

JULIUS and Livia settled down happily at their mother's feet. She was going to tell them their favourite story. They had heard it many times before, but they still enjoyed being told how their city, Rome, had been founded many years ago. This is what she said.

'Long ago and in a faraway country lived Venus. She was the goddess of love and beauty. She had a son called Aeneas. She was very proud of him. He had fought bravely in defending his city, Troy, against its enemies.

'But when Troy was captured, Aeneas had to flee for his life. He made a long voyage by land and sea and eventually reached the beautiful plain of Latium in Italy. Here he married the King's daughter and founded a kingdom of his own.

'Many, many years passed, and the kingdom entered troubled times. Numitor, one of Aeneas' descendants, was now King. His daughter Rhea had just given birth to twin sons called Romulus and Remus. Their father was Mars, the mighty god of war. It should have been a happy time for Numitor. But his wicked brother Amulius wanted his kingdom and drove Numitor out of the country.

'Amulius ordered his soldiers to throw the babies Romulus and Remus into the River Tiber. But the babies didn't drown. They were washed ashore. A she-wolf heard them crying, took them away and cared for them alongside her cubs. Later they were discovered by a shepherd, who carried the boys home and looked after them as if they were his own children.

'The boys grew up strong and brave, and with their help their grandfather, King Numitor, won back his throne from his brother.

'Romulus then began to build a city of his own. He chose a place where the River Tiber could be crossed, surrounded by seven hills overlooking the river. But Remus made fun of him and the city he was building. The twins fought each other and Remus was killed. But Romulus carried on building. And when he finished his city he became its first King. The city was called Rome.

'After reigning as King for forty years, Romulus mysteriously disappeared in the darkness of a great storm and became a god.'

◀ **SOURCE 1**
Drawing of a Roman coin from AD120

1. Which scene from the story do Sources 1 and 2 illustrate?
2. Find three things in the story that you think might be true.
3. Find three things in the story which you think are unlikely to be true.
4. Find out what things other people in the class have chosen. Then discuss whether Sources 1 and 2 prove that the story is true.
5. What does the fact that the Romans made the objects in Sources 1 and 2 tell us about the story?
6. Teachers and parents told this story to Roman children. What do you think they wanted them to learn from it? Here are some suggestions:
   ■ Romans are descended from gods. The gods like the Romans.
   ■ Good Romans should be loyal to their city and be prepared to kill for it.
   Now add your own ideas.

Activity

This story would make a good cartoon strip. Draw a strip with five frames. First of all choose what you think are the five most important scenes from the story. Then draw a picture and write a caption for each scene.

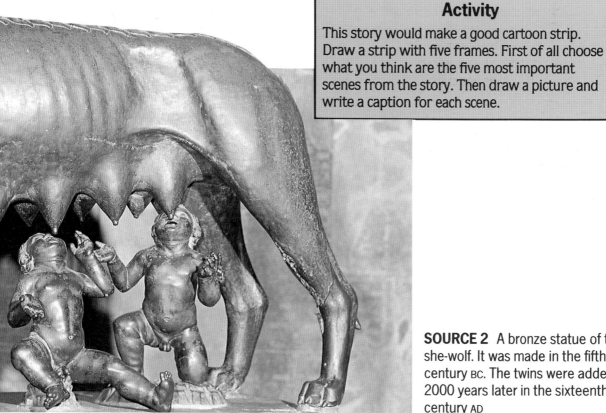

SOURCE 2 A bronze statue of the she-wolf. It was made in the fifth century BC. The twins were added 2000 years later in the sixteenth century AD

We do not know how much of the story of Romulus and Remus is true. We do know that around 753BC there were some villages on the seven hills overlooking the River Tiber. The people who lived there were called the Latins. The villages were gradually combined to form a city called Rome.

This city grew in importance until it controlled the whole of Italy, and later the whole of the land around the Mediterranean Sea.

We are going to look at two important moments (or turning points) in Rome's history – moments when Rome won decisive victories that allowed it to become more powerful.

Turning point 1 – the defeat of the Etruscans

The first kings of Rome were not Romans. They came from a TRIBE called the Etruscans. In the sixth century BC the Romans drove out the Etruscan King, Tarquin the Proud. He had been a harsh and unpopular ruler and the Romans were determined never to have a King again. Instead they set up a Republic, which meant that the citizens of Rome elected their rulers for just a year at a time.

It wasn't only the Etruscans who were troubling the Romans. Other neighbouring tribes, who wanted to capture the Romans' rich farming land, were always making raids.

To start with, the Romans only fought to defend themselves. But as they grew stronger and better at fighting they realised that attack was better than defence. They began to defeat the neighbouring tribes and take over their lands. Some tribes were wiped out, others surrendered and became allies. By 250BC, the Romans controlled the whole of Italy.

Turning point 2 – war with Carthage

Across the Mediterranean Sea, just a few hundred miles away, lay the great North African city of Carthage. You can see the CARTHAGINIAN EMPIRE marked on Source 4.

The Carthaginians traded all over the Mediterranean. The Romans were trying to expand their trade, but the Carthaginians treated the Roman traders as pirates and sank their ships. The Carthaginians also controlled much of Sicily – an

▼ **SOURCE 3** A Roman warship

island only a few miles off the coast of Italy – which was a fertile corn-growing area. It was only a matter of time before Rome went to war against Carthage.

The Romans had become skilful soldiers during their conquest of Italy. They had a large army of 100,000 soldiers. But they were faced with an enemy which had an excellent navy. To win the war, the Romans had to win control of the sea. They had no navy and little experience as sailors. However, they began building a huge battle fleet.

They also invented new tactics. On each ship they built a kind of drawbridge, called a *corvus*, with a huge iron spike on the end. The *corvus* stood upright by the mast. When an enemy ship was close it was lowered so that the spike sank into the enemy's deck. The Roman soldiers then charged across onto the enemy ship.

With the new navy, Rome managed to capture Sicily. The war with Carthage seemed to be over.

But peace did not last long. Hannibal, the leading Carthaginian general, intended to defeat the Romans once and for all. He planned a daring attack on Rome itself.

Hannibal was a determined and skilful general. When he was only nine years old his father had made him swear to be always an enemy of Rome. In 218BC Hannibal set out with an army of nearly 100,000 troops and 36 elephants.

---

1. Look at Source 3. Match up these captions with the numbers on the picture:
   - look-out tower
   - oars
   - a battering ram just out of sight below the surface of the water
   - soldiers with spears and shields
   - mascot – a crocodile, showing that this boat had fought successfully in the Nile.
2. How would each feature be useful in battle?
3. No drawing of a *corvus* has survived. Using the information given above, draw what you think it would have looked like.

Activity

You are a general in the Roman army. The government in Rome (called the Senate) has asked you to write a short report on Hannibal.

They want to know if you think he presents any danger to Rome.

Use the information in Source 4 to help you write your report. Mention:
- how Hannibal might try to get to Rome
- the obstacles in his way
- the size of his army compared with the Roman army
- whether you think he can succeed.

SOURCE 4 Hannibal's route to Rome, and the obstacles in his way

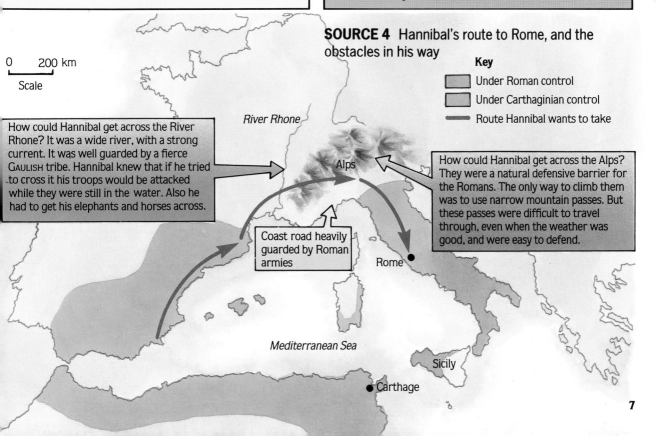

Key
- Under Roman control
- Under Carthaginian control
- Route Hannibal wants to take

0   200 km
Scale

How could Hannibal get across the River Rhone? It was a wide river, with a strong current. It was well guarded by a fierce GAULISH tribe. Hannibal knew that if he tried to cross it his troops would be attacked while they were still in the water. Also he had to get his elephants and horses across.

River Rhone

Alps

How could Hannibal get across the Alps? They were a natural defensive barrier for the Romans. The only way to climb them was to use narrow mountain passes. But these passes were difficult to travel through, even when the weather was good, and were easy to defend.

Coast road heavily guarded by Roman armies

Rome

Mediterranean Sea

Sicily

Carthage

The Romans were sure that they were safe from Hannibal. But they were wrong. The information on this page tells you how Hannibal dealt with the obstacles in his way(see Source 4 on the previous page).

The River Rhone

Hannibal first sent a small advance force of his best soldiers to cross the river secretly.

Hannibal then filled small boats and canoes with the light soldiers. The large boats were placed upstream of the light boats to protect them from the full force of the current.

Horses were towed behind the boats. One man on each side of the stern guided the horses.

As they crossed, the GAULISH tribesmen poured out of their camp – just as Hannibal had expected. But Hannibal's advance party rushed in to attack them and the tribesmen ran away.

The elephants then crossed, on huge rafts covered with earth and grass.

The Alps and the Allobrogians

Hannibal could not march along the well guarded coast road to Italy. So he took the only possible route, over the Alps, even though it was winter.

The Allobrogian tribe, who were friends of the Romans, had a large army in a strong position overlooking the Carthaginians' route down from the mountains.

Hannibal ordered the fires to be lit in his camp. He left most of his army there. He led his best soldiers to ambush the Allobrogians.

Up on the Alps the snow was already falling heavily. Hannibal saw that his men were in low spirits, because they had suffered much. To cheer them up, he called them together and pointed out Italy, which lay close beneath the mountains. The path down was very narrow and steep.

It was a treacherous path. Neither the soldiers nor the animals could tell where they were treading in the deep snow. Those that stepped wide of the path fell down the cliff to certain death.

Hannibal got his soldiers to cut a path out of the snow. After a day the path was wide enough for the packhorses and animals. It took three days to get the elephants through.

SOURCE 5 Hannibal's army crossing the Alps, drawn in the nineteenth century

SOURCE 6 Roman coin showing a war elephant

SOURCE 7 Written by the Roman historian Polybius, 300 years after the events

The elephants were of great use to the Carthaginians. The enemy were too terrified of their appearance to come anywhere near them. 99

Look at Sources 5, 6 and 7.
1. Why was Hannibal so keen to take war elephants with him?
2. What problems did the elephants cause for Hannibal?

Hannibal had started his campaign with 100,000 soldiers; 60,000 climbed the Alps with him, but only 23,000 reached Italy. Hannibal knew his army might not be strong enough to attack Rome, and he had no siege engines. He marched south until he was within three days' march of Rome. The people of Rome were nervous, but didn't panic. They waited.

Hannibal decided against attack. Instead he continued south, looking for supplies and trying to persuade the people of other cities to join him against Rome.

Hannibal is defeated

Hannibal spent the next fifteen years in Italy. The Romans sent a number of armies to fight him, but he defeated them every time. Finally the Romans changed their tactics. Instead of fighting him, they decided to wear him down. They stopped any extra soldiers or supplies getting through to him and they refused to fight any more big battles.

Hannibal's army grew weaker with every year that passed. He had already decided that he was not strong enough to attack Rome, and few of the Italian tribes joined him. They all stayed loyal to Rome.

Meanwhile, the Roman army concentrated its efforts on attacking Carthage. After fifteen years in Italy, Hannibal was ordered home to help defend Carthage from the Romans.

Activity
You are one of Hannibal's soldiers. You have just heard that you are being called home from Italy. You are writing to your family at home in Carthage, to explain why the campaign has failed.
a) Do you think Hannibal is a good general? Tell them how he crossed the obstacles which were in the way of the army. Did he do well?
b) Should he have taken the elephants? Some people are grumbling that the elephants have held you up.
c) Some people are saying he should not have climbed the Alps during the winter. What do you think?
d) Others say he should have attacked Rome straight away. What do you think?

In 202BC, near Carthage, Hannibal was defeated by the Roman general Scipio. The Carthaginians were beaten. Their lands in southern Spain were taken by Rome. Fifty years later, the city of Carthage itself was totally destroyed, and its North African lands were also taken by Rome.

Rome was now the strongest power around the Mediterranean Sea, and her Empire grew rapidly. In the 70 years after the defeat of Hannibal, Macedonia (now south-east Europe), Greece and Asia Minor (part of modern Turkey) came under Roman rule. Egypt was under Rome's influence.

Some countries that the Romans conquered became PROVINCES. New Roman towns called COLONIES were established. Other neighbouring countries became allies. The defeat of Carthage meant that Rome was the master of the whole Mediterranean area. But as we shall see, the Romans still found it difficult to control all these lands.

1. Historians see Hannibal's defeat as a major turning point in Rome's history. How did the defeat of Hannibal change things for Rome?

How was Rome governed?

AFTER the Romans threw out the hated Etruscan King, Tarquin the Proud, they were determined not to allow one man to become so powerful again. Instead, they wanted to choose the people who would govern them. They developed a new kind of government which they called *res publica* which meant 'a matter for the people'. See if you think Roman government was really 'a matter for the people'.

▼ **SOURCE 1** The Republic

RES PUBLICA – THE REPUBLIC

THE CITIZENS OF ROM
Divided into two classes

The PATRICIANS (nobles who owned large estates and were descended from the founders of the city)

They all met in the ASSEMBLY
Here they elected

elected

elected

el

TWO CONSULS governed the city. They were elected for one year only and could not be elected again until 10 years had passed. They both had to agree before a decision could be made

THE MAGISTRATES
Officials who were appointed to be judges, to look after the city's finances and other jobs

advised

retired

THE SENATE. When magistrates retired they became members of the senate. They had a lot of experience and gave advice to the CONSULS. THE SENATE became very important and ended up controlling Rome.

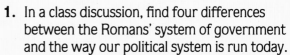

When the Romans spoke of 'the people' they meant Roman CITIZENS. This did not include the many slaves in Rome, most of whom were prisoners of war. Nor did it include women.

■ Only Roman citizens were able to vote.
■ Only Roman citizens could be elected into government jobs.
■ All Roman citizens were expected to fight in the army when needed.

1. In a class discussion, find four differences between the Romans' system of government and the way our political system is run today.
2. How did the Romans make sure that no one man could become too powerful?
3. When Hannibal was invading Italy, the rulers of Rome had to make quick decisions.
a) Can you think of any features of the Roman system that would have made it difficult to reach quick decisions?
b) Can you think of changes that might make quick decisions easier in times of emergency?

The PLEBEIANS (ordinary peasant farmers and craftsmen)

In reality, Patricians and Plebeians were never equal, even though they had equal rights. The Plebeians had to work, while many of the Patricians — who were very rich — had slaves and servants. This meant they could spend their time on politics. The result was that most of the magistrates and senators were Patricians.

All Roman citizens served in the army. As Rome conquered more territory, soldiers spent more time away from Italy. Many of the Patricians led Roman armies in the wars and returned home even richer, with many valuables from the conquered lands.

The Plebeians, however, were just ordinary soldiers. They returned from the fighting to find their farms in ruins. They were forced to sell their land to the rich, and drifted into Rome to live in the crowded slums. The government tried to keep them happy with hand-outs of free bread, but there were sometimes very bad riots.

TRIBUNES were appointed to protect the ordinary people against unfair treatment

Activity

It is 133BC. A tribune called Tiberius Gracchus has suggested that the big estates of the Patricians should be divided up. The land should be shared out between the poor, who would then farm it.

Gracchus' idea is going to be debated in the Assembly.

Carry out this debate in your classroom. One person will be Gracchus. Other people will be Patricians and Plebeians. There might also be some women arguing that they should have a say.
a) What are the Patricians' arguments for keeping things as they are?
b) What are the Plebeians' arguments for sharing out the land?
c) What are the women's arguments for being involved in making decisions?

Did the Republic work?

The Republic under threat

IN THE first century BC, Rome was faced with many problems (see Source 1).

▼ **SOURCE 1** Map of the Roman Empire in 100BC

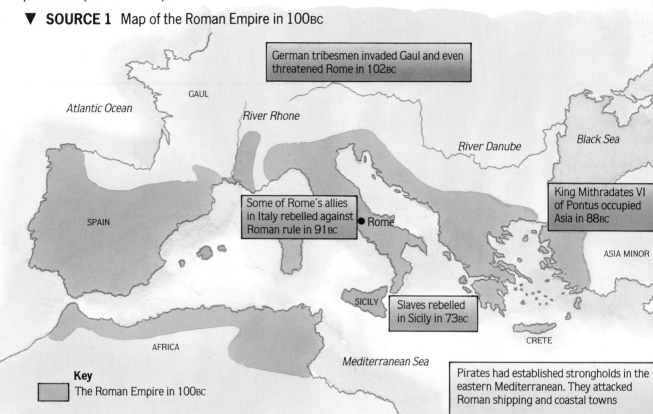

German tribesmen invaded Gaul and even threatened Rome in 102BC

GAUL

Atlantic Ocean

River Rhone

River Danube

Black Sea

King Mithradates VI of Pontus occupied Asia in 88BC

SPAIN

Some of Rome's allies in Italy rebelled against Roman rule in 91BC

● Rome

ASIA MINOR

SICILY

Slaves rebelled in Sicily in 73BC

CRETE

AFRICA

Mediterranean Sea

Key
The Roman Empire in 100BC

Pirates had established strongholds in the eastern Mediterranean. They attacked Roman shipping and coastal towns

Rome depended on army generals like Pompey and Julius Caesar to deal with threats to Rome. They had been successful in dealing with the problems in Source 1.

The two men were friends at first, but they became deadly rivals as each tried to become more powerful than the other.

SOURCE 2

POMPEY
■ had cleared pirates out of the Mediterranean
■ had won back Asia Minor (modern Turkey)
■ had conquered Syria and Palestine
■ had the support of the Senate.

SOURCE 3

CAESAR
■ had led his army to conquer the whole of GAUL
■ had sent an expedition over to Britain
■ was a popular hero with his troops and with the ordinary people of Rome.

Arguments broke out over how Rome should be governed. Some Romans were beginning to think that Rome would be safer if one of these generals took over completely. They thought that the Republic wasn't very good at dealing with the problems Rome faced.

BC 218BC 44BC AD500

The SENATE disliked Caesar and supported Pompey (we'll see why very soon), and ordered Caesar to get rid of his army. Caesar ignored them, and in 48BC defeated Pompey in battle.

Most ordinary Romans were quite happy to let Caesar take over as 'DICTATOR for life', even though he had not been elected.

But this did not last very long. Sources 4 and 5 tell you what happened next.

SOURCE 5 Caesar's murder, painted in the nineteenth century

The murderers were all SENATORS. Most of them were Caesar's enemies, but they also included Brutus, whom Caesar was very fond of and who may even have been Caesar's son.

> **SOURCE 4** Written by the Roman historian Suetonius, about 175 years after the events
>
> 66 *As Caesar took his seat in the Senate, the conspirators gathered about him as if to pay their respects. One of them, Casca, stabbed him just below the throat. As Caesar tried to leap to his feet, he was stopped by another wound. When he saw that he was beset on every side by daggers, he muffled his head in his robe. He was stabbed 23 times.* 99

Why did they murder Caesar?

Many different explanations have been given for why the senators murdered Caesar:
- They thought he was becoming too powerful.
- Some thought he wanted to become King, and that would mean the end of the Republic.
- Some of the senators were jealous of him.
- The senators disliked Caesar because he was arrogant and acted as though he was superior.
- The Senate was worried that he was on the side of the Plebeians and wanted to make the Senate less powerful.

Now read Sources 6–12, which tell you more about Julius Caesar.

SOURCE 6 Some of Caesar's actions that had made him popular with the poor

- *Caesar helped the unemployed by selling them land cheaply.*
- *He provided building work in Rome.*
- *He made taxes fairer.*

SOURCE 7 From Cicero's letters. Cicero was an important Roman politician

a) Written after Julius Caesar had been to stay with him

> 66 *Julius Caesar was not the sort of guest to whom you would say, 'Please come again on the way back'. Once is enough. . . . He refused to talk to me about matters of government. . . . I found it a bother to entertain him.* 99

b) Written after Caesar ignored the rules for appointing consuls

> 66 *At one o'clock in the afternoon, Caesar announced the election of a consul to serve until 1 January, which was the very next morning . . . . You laugh. If you were here you'd weep. What if I told you everything? There were countless similar incidents.* 99

13

SOURCE 8 The Roman writer Suetonius records the senators' criticism of Caesar

66 *He accepted excessive honours. He became consul several times and dictator for life. He accepted honours that should only be given to a god: a gold throne, statues beside those of the gods, a special priest, and one of the months of the year was named after him.*

At the Latin Festival someone placed on his statue a laurel wreath with a white ribbon tied to it [the white ribbon was the sign of a King]. The tribunes gave orders that the ribbon be removed, but Caesar told them off. From that time on he could not get rid of the rumours that he wanted to be King. 99

SOURCE 9 Written by the Greek historian Cassius Dio, about 270 years after the events

66 *Caesar pardoned those who warred against him [in the war with Pompey] and gained a great reputation, both for bravery and for goodness.* 99

SOURCE 10 Written by the Greek writer Plutarch, about 150 years after the events

66 *It was unthinkable that Caesar would ever do so great a crime as destroy the Roman Republic.* 99

SOURCE 11 Suetonius makes his own judgement

66 *It was the following action that caused the deadly hatred of the Senate against him: when they approached him he refused to rise.* 99

SOURCE 12 Some rumours about Caesar which were going around in Rome

66 ■ *He planned to move the capital of the Empire to Egypt.*
■ *He had ordered many opponents to be beheaded, or whipped to death, and he'd burned their homes.*
■ *He put his statue among the statues of kings.*
■ *He had love affairs with many men and women.* 99

1. Read Sources 6–12. Decide whether any of the sources support or contradict the reasons for Caesar's murder given on page 13.
2. Do Sources 6–12 suggest any other reasons for Caesar's murder?
3. Working with a partner, decide which of the reasons is the most important. List them in order of importance. If two reasons seem equally important, put them side by side.
4. The picture in Source 5 is going to be used in a book about Caesar. You have been asked to write an explanation of Caesar's murder to go with the picture. In a headline and a single paragraph explain why you think the senators murdered Caesar.

The end of the Republic?

The people were outraged at Caesar's murder. The citizens of Rome took matters into their own hands. They gave Caesar's body a grand public cremation in the centre of the city, and then ran riot. They chased the murderers out of Rome, killed some of them and burned their houses.

Caesar left the vast majority of his wealth to his adopted son Octavian. But when Caesar's will was read out in public the citizens of Rome found they had each been left money.

If the murderers of Caesar had hoped for a return to the REPUBLIC, they were disappointed. Only months later, Octavian (who was only eighteen years old), helped by his supporters (including many soldiers loyal to Caesar), marched on Rome. They were determined to take revenge on Caesar's murderers. In the next five years 300 senators and 2000 other citizens were executed. In 42BC the last republican leaders, Brutus and Cassius, were defeated in battle.

Octavian was too clever to abolish the Republic and declare himself EMPEROR. But most historians agree that the Republic was ended, and that Octavian – who was given a new name, Augustus – was the first Emperor. The Roman Republic had become the Roman Empire.

See if you agree. Read the following sources and then answer the questions that follow.

SOURCE 13 Augustus ordered these things to be inscribed outside his grave for everybody to read

In my sixth and seventh consulships, after I had stamped out the civil wars, and at a time when I was in absolute control of everything, I transferred the Republic from my own control to the Senate and the people of Rome.

SOURCE 14 Some of the things that a biography by Suetonius says about Augustus

■ *He first took the consulship by leading his armies against Rome and sending soldiers as messengers to demand the office for him. When the Senate hesitated, one of the soldiers threw back his cloak, and showing the hilt of his sword said, 'This will make him consul, if you do not'.*
■ *He thought of restoring the Republic but he decided it would be dangerous to share power between several people.*

SOURCE 15 Written by a modern historian

The Plebeians continued to re-elect Augustus as consul every year. His popularity with them was overwhelming and gave him all the powers he needed.

SOURCE 16 In 27BC, after Augustus handed back power to the Senate, the Senate passed a law giving the power back to him

. . . that he might have the right and power to do whatever he shall judge to be in the best interests of the state.

1. According to Source 14, how did Augustus become consul?
2. Did Augustus give back power to the Senate and people of Rome?
3. According to Source 13, why could Augustus not have done this earlier?
4. Why might the Plebeians keep on electing Augustus as consul?

AUGUSTUS

He sent soldiers to the senate to demand the office of consul for him.

The Plebeians re-elected Augustus as consul thirteen times.

A journey through Rome

UNDER Augustus the Roman Empire continued to grow. As it grew, Rome changed. The earliest Romans had been proud of their simple life. They worked hard. They were all willing to join the army when Rome was in danger. But the Empire quickly changed all that. Conquests brought great wealth to Rome. Many goods were imported, and large numbers of slaves were used to do all the hard work. All these things meant that life in Rome changed a great deal.

Augustus made many changes to Rome. He thought that the city was not as great as the capital of the Empire should be. He boasted that he found Rome built of sun-dried bricks and left it built of marble.

He built many public buildings. To guard against fires he employed night-watchmen, and to control floods he widened and cleared the River Tiber which had been full of rubbish.

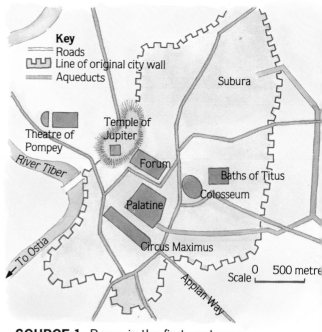

SOURCE 1 Rome in the first century AD

Activity

What would Rome have looked like if you had visited it in the first century AD?

You are a merchant from the town of Wroxeter in far-away Britain. Sources 2–20 show you what you would have seen on your visit to Rome.

Read through pages 16–21, answering the questions as you go along. As you read about your visit to Rome, mark your route on your own copy of the map in Source 1.

You have arrived in Ostia, the port of Rome, on a cargo ship carrying wine and pottery from Gaul. The port is about 25 kilometres from Rome.

SOURCE 2 Written by the writer Aelius Aristides in the second century AD

> So many merchant ships arrive in Rome with cargoes from everywhere, at all times of the year, that the city seems like the world's warehouse. The arrival and departure of ships never stops – it's amazing that the sea, not to mention the harbour, is big enough for all these merchant ships.

You could take a ferry boat to the centre of Rome but you have had enough of boats. You decide to hire a carriage called a *raeda* (see Source 3).

SOURCE 3 A carving of a carriage

Your journey takes you along the Appian Way to the outskirts of the city. Rome has grown rapidly. It now has well over a million people, mostly living outside the lines of the original city wall. As your carriage drives along the Appian Way, you are surprised to see tombstones lining the road (see Source 4).

Your carriage is now in a built-up area. Ahead, you can see the remains of the old city wall. Your carriage is not allowed into the city during daylight, so your driver stops at an inn by the Appian Gate. You pay your fare and have a drink at the tavern. Then, as the afternoon gets cooler, you set out for a walk through the centre of the city.

The streets are lined with houses, blocks of flats, shops and workshops. You stop to look at these as you pass by (see Sources 7 and 8).

SOURCE 4 Tombstones on the Appian Way

SOURCE 5 Written by Paulus, a law writer, about AD200

It is not allowed to bring a corpse into a city, in case the sacred places of the city become polluted. A corpse cannot be buried or cremated within the city.

SOURCE 7 A workshop: a cobbler and a rope-maker at work

SOURCE 6 Inscription on a tombstone by the Appian Way

Stranger, my message is short. Stand here and read it. Here is the unlovely tomb of a lovely woman. Her parents gave her the name of Claudia. She loved her husband with all her heart. She had two sons, one of whom she buried. She was charming to talk to and gentle to be with. She looked after the house and spun wool. That's my last word. Go on your way.

SOURCE 8 A shop

1. Historians get much of their information about people in the Roman Empire from inscriptions on tombs. Write down three facts the tombstone tells us about Claudia.

Study Source 8 carefully.
2. What is being sold in the shop?
3. How are the goods displayed?
4. Which do you think are the customers and which is the shopkeeper? Explain your answer.

DRAWING BY ALAN SORRELL

SOURCE 9 Reconstruction of a street scene in Rome

SOURCE 10 Written by the humorous writer Juvenal in the second century AD

❝*The fear of fires, the constant collapse of houses, the thousand dangers of a cruel city.*

However fast we hurry, there's a huge crowd ahead and a mob behind pushing and shoving. You get dug in the ribs by someone's elbow. Then someone hits you with a long pole, another with a beam from a building or a wine-barrel.

The streets are filthy — your legs are plastered with mud. A soldier's hob-nailed boot lands right on your toe. Togas which have just been patched are torn. A great trunk of a fir tree sways in its rumbling waggon and totters menacingly over the heads of the crowd.❞

1. Which things in Source 9 could have been reconstructed from ARCHAEOLOGICAL evidence?
2. Which things in the drawing could not have been reconstructed from archaeological evidence?
3. How could historians find out these things?
4. Which gives you the best impression of what it was like in the streets of Rome: Source 9 or Source 10? Explain your answer.

As you walk towards the centre of the city, you notice a huge arch crossing high above the streets (see Source 9). This is one of the AQUEDUCTS that bring water supplies into Rome. This one was repaired by Augustus. It takes water directly into the Palatine, which is where the Emperor lives.

At last you reach the centre of Rome. Here are all the important public buildings.

You arrive at a huge public bath-house. There are many of these in the city. These baths are used by everybody, rich and poor alike. They are cheap, and children are allowed in free. Romans spend hours there chatting with friends and conducting business, as well as bathing.

However they can be rather a nuisance if you live near one. Source 11 is what a Roman poet, Lucius Seneca, wrote about them in the first century AD.

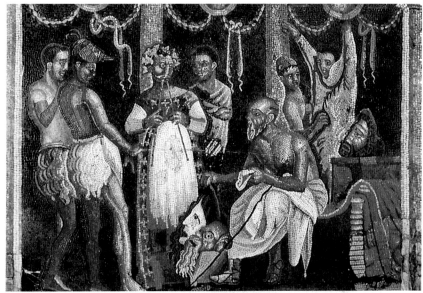

SOURCE 13 First-century mosaic showing actors at the theatre

You find somewhere to stay for the night in Subura, a busy area of Rome with many shops, taverns and flats. Late in the evening the streets are still teeming with people and very noisy. And when you go to bed for the night, the noise from the street outside seems to get worse, not better!

SOURCE 11

I live over the public baths. It's sickening. First, there are the 'strongmen' doing their exercises and swinging heavy lead weights about with grunts and groans. Next, the lazy ones, having a cheap massage. I can hear someone being slapped on the shoulders. Then there is the man who likes the sound of his own voice in the bath. And what about the ones who leap into the pool, making a huge splash?

SOURCE 14 Written by Juvenal

How can anyone sleep in lodgings here? It's only the rich who get any sleep. The noise of the carts thundering along the narrow streets, and the language of the drivers when they get stuck in a traffic jam, would wake even the heaviest sleeper.

But the baths are not the only building for leisure and entertainment. Back in Britain some towns have a theatre, but here there are several to choose from. The Emperor Nero loved performances in a small theatre called an *odeon*. In fact, he used to perform himself (see Source 12).

SOURCE 15 A recent account of life in Augustus' Rome

No traffic was allowed in the centre of Rome during the day, so . . . as night fell, the darkened streets became crowded with cattle going to market, people moving house, people emptying out the cess pits, farmers with their carts carrying oil and wine to deliver to the shops, animal cages on the way to the circus, soldiers moving military supplies.

SOURCE 12 Written by the Roman historian Suetonius

It was forbidden to leave the theatre during a recital by Nero – however urgent the reason – and the gates were kept locked. Women in the audience gave birth, and some of the men were so bored that they pretended to be dead and were carried away to be buried.

---

5. Why do you think no heavy traffic was allowed in central Rome during the day?

A JOURNEY THROUGH ROME

In the morning you step out of your lodgings to find the streets deserted! This can only mean one thing. The chariot races are taking place at the Circus Maximus (see Source 16). As you get closer you can hear the roar of the crowd.

▼ **SOURCE 16** A drawing of the Circus Maximus. The stadium held 250,000 spectators, but not always safely. In the time of the Emperor Nero 13,000 people were killed in a single accident, when banks of seating collapsed

SOURCE 17 Pliny, a Roman writer, describes the chariot races. Four chariots raced each other seven times around the track (five miles). Each team wore different colours: the Reds, the Blues, the Greens and the Whites

" If you've seen one race you've seen them all. I cannot understand why so many thousands want to see chariots racing. Why don't they grow up? I wouldn't mind, if they went to see the skill of the charioteers. But all they support is the colour of the driver's tunic. If they swapped colours in mid-race, I swear they'd follow the colours and change their support too.

On the next day, you see the Colosseum, a vast AMPITHEATRE, where GLADIATORS and wild animals from all around the Empire fight to the death. You have seen gladiators in Britain, but nothing on this scale. The Colosseum holds 50,000 spectators and the shows go on for weeks! (See page 50.)

1. Before you leave Rome you are going to visit one of the entertainments – the baths, the chariot racing, the theatre or the gladiator fights. Look back at all the information on pages 16–21. Which do you choose, and why? Mark the route to the entertainment you choose on your map.

Now it is time for you to complete the business you came to Rome to discuss. The Romans might discuss business matters at the baths, or even at the public toilets (see Source 18), but you go to the heart of Rome – the Forum (see Source 19). This is an enormous area full of magnificent buildings which are all used for government or religion.

At the centre of the Forum is the Temple of Julius Caesar. It is built over the spot where his body was cremated.

SOURCE 18 A public toilet. There were a large number of public toilets, like this one, in Rome. The toilet became a meeting place for Romans, where business or politics could be discussed, or gossip exchanged

SOURCE 19 An artist's reconstruction of the Forum. The huge building on the left is the Basilica, Rome's business centre

SOURCE 20 Written by the architect Vitruvius in 27BC

In the Forum both public and private business is controlled by the town's officials. The site of the Basilica should be fixed next to the Forum in as warm an area as possible so that in winter businessmen may meet there without being troubled by the weather.

Like most people in the Roman Empire, you believe that your life is controlled by gods and goddesses. You make regular offerings (gifts) to the gods at home to earn their approval so that your business will do well. Today, your last day in Rome, you decide to make an offering in the Temple of Jupiter (the King of the gods). You walk up a hill to reach it. From the top you can see many other temples. All the main gods have at least one temple in Rome.

It is time for you to leave Rome. You take a Tiber ferry back to Ostia. On the way, you think back over your time in Rome.

1. When you get back home to Wroxeter, you are asked to produce a two-page leaflet advertising Rome as a good place to visit. Choose features of Rome that would most appeal to Roman citizens living in the rest of the Empire. You can use words and pictures from this book.
2. Do you think that the attractions you have included in your leaflet would appeal to people today?

Life in Rome

SO FAR, you have been looking at Rome from the point of view of a visitor. But what was it like to live in Rome? That would depend a great deal on whether you were rich or poor.

Rome's success in conquering other countries made it a very wealthy city. But this just meant that the gap between the rich and the poor widened. Up on the hills around Rome were elegant mansions owned by the rich. In the city itself were street after street of ramshackle blocks of flats. Almost all of Rome's one million people lived cramped into these poorly-built blocks.

1. Source 3 shows two blocks of flats. Can you see the following:
   - the rich family
   - their slave cooking dinner
   - the poor families
   - the tavern?
2. Write two or more sentences summing up the contrasting living conditions of rich and poor Roman families living in blocks of flats.

SOURCE 1 Written by the Roman writer Juvenal in the first century AD

“*We live in a city shored up with slender props — for that's how the landlords stop the houses from falling down. I would like to live in a place that's free from fires and alarms.*”

SOURCE 2 Written by the politician and historian Tacitus in the first century AD

“*Rome has narrow winding alleyways, irregular streets with tall buildings where the sun never reaches.*”

▼ **SOURCE 3** An artist's reconstruction of flats in Rome

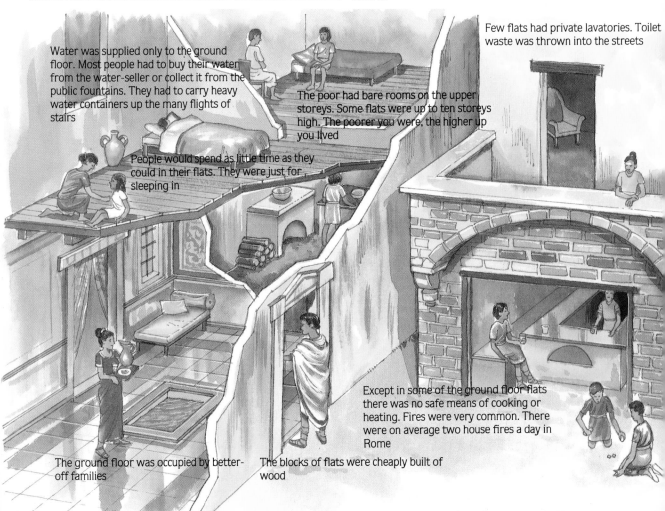

Water was supplied only to the ground floor. Most people had to buy their water from the water-seller or collect it from the public fountains. They had to carry heavy water containers up the many flights of stairs

Few flats had private lavatories. Toilet waste was thrown into the streets

The poor had bare rooms on the upper storeys. Some flats were up to ten storeys high. The poorer you were, the higher up you lived

People would spend as little time as they could in their flats. They were just for sleeping in

Except in some of the ground floor flats there was no safe means of cooking or heating. Fires were very common. There were on average two house fires a day in Rome

The ground floor was occupied by better-off families

The blocks of flats were cheaply built of wood

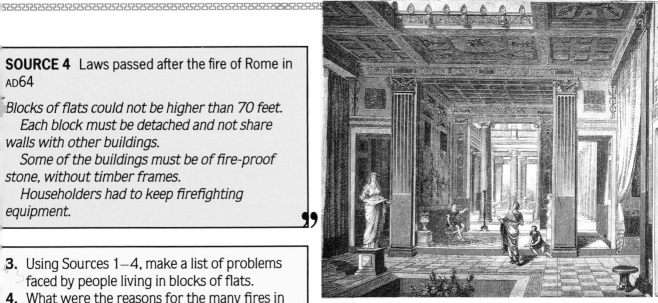

SOURCE 4 Laws passed after the fire of Rome in AD64

Blocks of flats could not be higher than 70 feet.
Each block must be detached and not share walls with other buildings.
Some of the buildings must be of fire-proof stone, without timber frames.
Householders had to keep firefighting equipment. **"**

SOURCE 6 An artist's reconstruction of the inside

3. Using Sources 1–4, make a list of problems faced by people living in blocks of flats.
4. What were the reasons for the many fires in Rome? Why did the fires spread so easily?
5. Do you think the measures described in Source 4 would be helpful? What other actions could the authorities take to solve the problem?

6. Pick three features of Sources 5 and 6 that you would not expect to find in an English house today, and explain why they were popular in first-century Italy.
7. Describe any similarities between the houses and living conditions in Sources 1–6 and houses or flats that you know today.

Outside the city centre, on the hills overlooking Rome, stood the grand mansions of the richest Romans. Sources 5 and 6 show what ARCHAEOLOGISTS believe these looked like.

▼ **SOURCE 5** Floor plan and external view of a Roman mansion

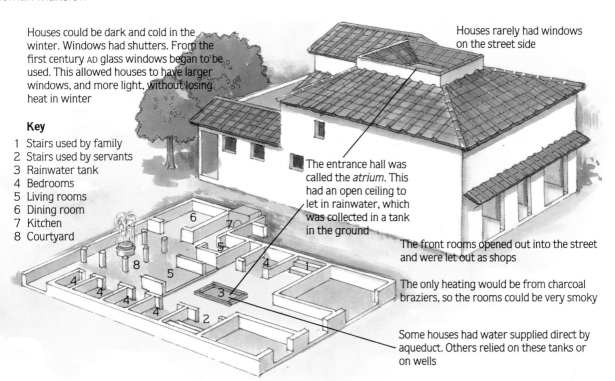

Houses could be dark and cold in the winter. Windows had shutters. From the first century AD glass windows began to be used. This allowed houses to have larger windows, and more light, without losing heat in winter

Houses rarely had windows on the street side

Key
1 Stairs used by family
2 Stairs used by servants
3 Rainwater tank
4 Bedrooms
5 Living rooms
6 Dining room
7 Kitchen
8 Courtyard

The entrance hall was called the *atrium*. This had an open ceiling to let in rainwater, which was collected in a tank in the ground

The front rooms opened out into the street and were let out as shops

The only heating would be from charcoal braziers, so the rooms could be very smoky

Some houses had water supplied direct by aqueduct. Others relied on these tanks or on wells

Family life

The Roman family was often bigger than most modern British families. For rich families, it included not only the mother, father and children, but also other relatives living in the house and all the household slaves. The father was head of the family. He had power over everybody in his house, from his wife to his slaves.

The life women led depended a lot on their social status. Wealthy women often had a lot of independence, especially if they were widows. Women could own and inherit property, and a few wealthy women managed their own businesses. Many middle-class women shared the work in crafts and trades with their husbands, especially in silver-working and perfumery. Women could become priestesses, hairdressers or midwives, and there were some female doctors, but men kept most jobs to themselves.

At the other end of the scale, many women were slaves, doing jobs ranging from lady's maid to farmworker. Some were even GLADIATORS.

SOURCE 7 Inscription on a tombstone praising a 'perfect' wife

66 *Here lies Amyone, wife of Marcus. She was most good and beautiful, a spinner of wool, obedient, chaste and stay-at-home.* 99

SOURCE 8 A Roman writer describes the kind of wife he wouldn't like to have

66 *. . . a flatchested, straightfaced woman who dashes about all over town, turning up at all-male gatherings, telling the army generals in uniform just what to do — and all this while her husband is there as well.* 99

SOURCE 9 An account by a Roman writer of how women protested about a law which banned them from wearing colourful clothes and riding in carriages during wartime. The woman won and the law was abolished

66 *The women could not be kept indoors, either by the magistrates or their husbands. They blocked all the streets to the city and besieged the doors of the magistrates who were preventing the law being abolished.*

SOURCE 10 Painting of a Roman woman, from a coffin lid found in Egypt. The painting shows the woman as her relatives would like to remember her, but probably not as she was just before she died!

SOURCE 11 A woman innkeeper

1   2   3   4

SOURCE 12 A carving showing the stages in a boy's life:
. His mother feeds him
. His father carries him
. He rides on a miniature goat chariot
. He tells his father what he has learned at school

Women played the main role in bringing up the children. Roman parents were encouraged by the government to have large families, but most Romans hoped to have sons rather than daughters. In the fourth century, the SENATE had to pass a law forbidding people to leave newborn baby girls out in the open to die.

Boys in rich families were taught by tutors or went to school, but most children could not read or write. They were sent out to work at an early age.

SOURCE 13 Women slaves fighting as gladiators. Their stage names were Achillia and Amazon

SOURCE 14 A child's toy made of toxic lead

Study Sources 7–13 carefully.
1. What can they tell us about:
   a) what some men thought the perfect Roman wife should be like
   b) how women really behaved
   c) what parts of Roman life women were able to join in
   d) how important women were in family life?

2. What impression does Source 12 give you of the life of a child in Rome?
3. Divide into groups – if possible, some boys, some girls and some mixed.
   a) Use the evidence on these two pages to make statements on the status of women in first-century Rome. How different or similar is it to the situation in Britain nowadays?
   b) Compare your statements with other groups.

25

LIFE IN ROME

Food and diet

The poor did not have kitchens and could not do any cooking. If they could afford it, they bought hot food from one of the many bars in the streets.

Their diet was one of bread, wheatmeal porridge, beans, lentils and a little meat. Many poor Romans depended on free hand-outs to survive.

> **SOURCE 15** Extracts from Augustus' record of his own achievements
>
> 66 *In my eleventh year of power I gave free grain to at least 250,000 people.*
>
> *In my thirteenth year of power I gave free grain to 200,000 people.*
>
> *Whenever the government did not have enough money, I gave free grain from my own granary to over 100,000 people.* 99

For wealthy Romans, on the other hand, eating was a major part of a day's activity. The main meal started at about three o'clock in the afternoon and went on for several hours, with many courses. The meal was a social occasion and there would be entertainment between courses, such as dancers or gladiatorial fights.

The food was cooked and served by slaves.

People ate with their fingers. They drank wine, which was usually mixed with water.

Olives were often eaten as a first course.

Fish was very popular, and stuffed dormice were regarded as a delicacy. There was not much meat on them, but that did not matter to the Romans, as they had lots of courses. A very strong-tasting sauce called *garum* was used to help cover up the taste of the fish and meat, which were often not very fresh. How the food looked was as important as how it tasted.

Fruits like figs and grapes were served for the dessert courses.

▶ **SOURCE 16** A modern reconstruction of the kitchen in a Roman house

> **SOURCE 17** The recipe for the writer Cicero's favourite meal
>
> 66 *Take the flesh of a large salt water fish, filleted. Mix it with brains, chicken's liver, hard-boiled eggs and cheese. Sprinkle it with a sauce of pepper, honey and oil and then cook it in oil over a slow fire. Finally bind it together with raw eggs.*

> 1. Look at Source 16. Make a list of similarities and differences to a modern kitchen. Mention:
>   - how the food is cooked or heated
>   - how food is stored
>   - what the utensils are made of.

Shopping

At first, the main market in Rome was in the FORUM. When this became too crowded, new markets were built near to the River Tiber. There was a cattle market, a vegetable and fruit market and a fish market. As well as this, certain streets specialised in one kind of shop. But the great shopping street of Rome – the Street of the Etruscans – had shops and workshops of all sorts.

North of the Forum was the working-class district of Subura. It was full of small shops where the poor shopped.

Activity

Work in groups. Each group has to run the household of a rich Roman family and draw up a shopping list. There is going to be an important dinner party, and you have to stock up with the clothes and goods that the household needs.

First, identify the shops and workshops shown in Sources 18–22. Your teacher will give you clues if you need help. Then draw up a shopping list. Include at least five items that a rich household would need for a special meal like the ones described above, and five other general items you would need for the household. Alongside each item, show which shop you would buy this from (look back at Sources 7 and 8 on page 17 as well).

▲ SOURCE 18

▲ SOURCE 19

▲ SOURCE 20

▲ SOURCE 21

▲ SOURCE 22

How was Rome fed and supplied?

IN 50BC most of what Rome needed still came from Italy itself. But the city was growing rapidly, and 100 years later the situation had changed.

SOURCE 1 Written by Aelius Aristoides about Rome in the first century AD

"Egypt, Sicily and the civilised parts of Africa are your farms."

---

1. Look at Source 1. What do you think the writer means?

---

2. Look at Source 2. Where did the following goods come from?
   - timber
   - wine
   - fishpaste
   - papyrus.
3. Did most goods come by water or by road?
4. Where is the nearest supplier of corn?
5. Which of the imports shown would be used for:
   - eating and cooking
   - building
   - clothing?

By the middle of the first century, most of what Rome needed was imported from various parts of its enormous EMPIRE. Italy did not produce goods of its own. Instead, the PROVINCES of the Empire either paid for Rome's supplies by taxes or supplied it with goods. Source 2 shows you how Rome was supplied in the first century AD.

▼ **SOURCE 2** Map showing the main goods and products supplied to Rome by the provinces in the first century AD

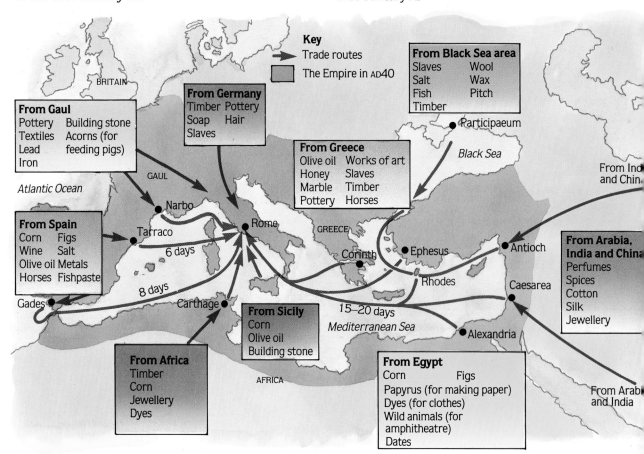

Key
→ Trade routes
The Empire in AD40

From Black Sea area
Slaves   Wool
Salt   Wax
Fish   Pitch
Timber

From Gaul
Pottery   Building stone
Textiles Acorns (for
Lead   feeding pigs)
Iron

From Germany
Timber   Pottery
Soap   Hair
Slaves

From Greece
Olive oil Works of art
Honey   Slaves
Marble   Timber
Pottery   Horses

From Spain
Corn   Figs
Wine   Salt
Olive oil Metals
Horses Fishpaste

From Arabia, India and China
Perfumes
Spices
Cotton
Silk
Jewellery

From Sicily
Corn
Olive oil
Building stone

From Africa
Timber
Corn
Jewellery
Dyes

From Egypt
Corn   Figs
Papyrus (for making paper)
Dyes (for clothes)
Wild animals (for amphitheatre)
Dates

BRITAIN
Atlantic Ocean
GAUL
Narbo
Tarraco
6 days
8 days
Gades
Carthage
AFRICA
Rome
GREECE
Corinth
Ephesus
Rhodes
15–20 days
Mediterranean Sea
Alexandria
Black Sea
Participaeum
Antioch
Caesarea
From India and China
From Arabia and India

Corn was the most important import. Most emperors tried to keep the poor people of Rome on their side by supplying cheap (or often free) corn. When they didn't do this they faced riots, and their position as Emperor might even be threatened. So vast amounts of corn were imported (see Source 3).

Most of this trade came through Ostia, which grew into a massive port with warehouses, customs offices, and ship-building yards.

Goods were then transported along the river or canal to Rome (see Source 5).

After the fire of AD94 there were so many ships carrying building materials that this route was almost completely blocked.

SOURCE 3 A corn ship, from a first-century wall painting

SOURCE 4 An antelope being loaded on board a ship bound for Rome. It is being taken to be killed in the amphitheatre

6. Look at this list of jobs done by Romans in the first century AD
   - barge workers
   - rope-makers
   - dock labourers
   - warehousemen
   - corn-measurers
   - cobblers
   - lawyers
   - doctors
   - brick-makers

a) Which of these jobs are being done in Sources 3–5?

b) Which of these jobs might need to be done at Ostia? Explain your answer.

SOURCE 5 Barges, towed by slaves, carrying a cargo of wine

Does Rome need another province?

IT IS AD43. You are the Emperor Claudius. Your position as Emperor is not secure. There has already been one attempted rebellion against you, and there is a shortage of grain in Rome.

As you can see from Source 2 on the previous page, GAUL has been conquered. It has been a Roman PROVINCE for 90 years. If the Empire is going to keep expanding, Britain is the obvious next step. Previous emperors thought the same. Augustus even raised an invasion army – but he had to put down a rebellion in Gaul and never got to Britain.

Now it's your turn. What should you do about Britain? Should you invade it?

There are a number of things you need to take into account to decide whether to invade:
- Can you keep up a profitable trade with Britain if you don't invade?
- Will an invasion be successful? Can you beat the Britons? A victory would do your reputation good. Every Emperor needs a military victory to help win support back in Rome.
- Will it be worth it financially? Are you likely to get more money in taxes from the Britons than it would cost you to keep Britain under control?
- Will it help security on your borders?
- Does Britain have resources that you want to exploit?

Sources 1–8 show some of the information you know about Britain. Read through them all and answer the questions before deciding whether to invade Britain.

---

1. Read Sources 1–4. What kind of place do the writers think Britain was?
2. Are some of the descriptions more reliable than others? Explain why.
3. What do the sources disagree about? Why do you think they disagree?
4. Write down three facts that Claudius would have known about Britain from Sources 1–4, and three opinions.

SOURCE 1 A description written in the first century BC by a Roman poet, Horace. He never visited Britain

❝Britain is at the very end of the earth. The Britons are savage towards foreigners. The seas around Britain are full of sea-monsters.❞

SOURCE 2 From Julius Caesar's accounts of his invasions of Britain in 55BC and in 54BC. He invaded because British tribes were helping the Gauls in their fight against Roman rule

❝All Britons dye themselves with woad, which produces a blue dye and makes them look wild in battle.

The population of Britain is very large, and there are many farmhouses. There is a large number of cattle. Most of the tribes living inland do not grow grain. They live on milk and meat and wear skins.

For coins they use bronze, gold or iron. Tin is found inland and small quantities of iron near the coast. The bronze they use is imported. There is timber of every kind.

The Britons' method of fighting is from chariots, dashing about all over the battle field hurling their spears. Our men were unnerved by these tactics, which were strange to them.

SOURCE 3 Written by the Roman politician Cicero at the time of Caesar's invasion. He had not been to Britain

❝We know there is not a trace of silver in the island, and that the only hope of plunder is slaves.

SOURCE 4 A description written 60 years after Caesar's invasion by the Greek writer Strabo. He did not visit Britain

❝Their way of life is a bit like that of the Gauls but much cruder and more barbaric. For example, although they have plenty of milk, some of them do not know how to make cheese. Nor do they know anything about farming.

They have more rain than snow, and on days when there is no rain the fog hangs about for so long that the sun shines for about three or four hours a day.

Grain, cattle, gold, silver and iron are found in Britain. They are exported with hides, slaves and excellent hunting dogs.

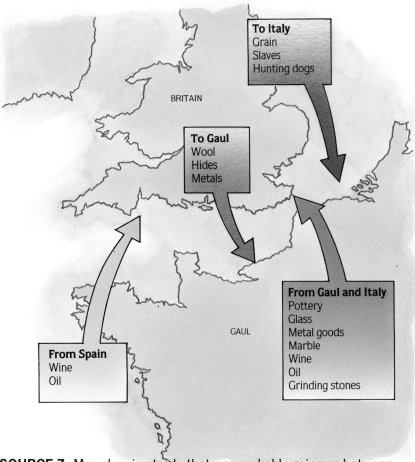

SOURCE 5 Two events in Britain in AD41

a) *Cunobelinus, chief of the Catuvellauni tribe, died. His sons were anti-Roman.*

b) *A Briton called Berikos was driven out of the island as a result of the civil war, and came to Rome to try to persuade Claudius to send a force to invade.* "

SOURCE 6 A Roman coin showing a picture of a Celtic chieftain that the Romans had defeated. The Celts were the people who lived in Britain and Gaul

Map labels:

To Italy
Grain
Slaves
Hunting dogs

BRITAIN

To Gaul
Wool
Hides
Metals

From Gaul and Italy
Pottery
Glass
Metal goods
Marble
Wine
Oil
Grinding stones

GAUL

From Spain
Wine
Oil

SOURCE 7 Map showing trade that was probably going on between Britain and the Roman Empire in AD40

SOURCE 8 Written by the historian Strabo just after Augustus had called off his planned invasion of Britain in 26BC

Although the Romans could have possessed Britain, they scorned to do so. They saw there was nothing at all to fear from the Britons, since they are not strong enough to cross over the ocean and attack us.

Some of the British chieftains have become friends to Augustus. They have made the island virtually a Roman possession.

The Britons are likely to put up with heavy duties on their imports and exports. There is no need to keep troops there.

It would require at least one legion [5000 soldiers] to collect taxes from them. The cost of the troops would be as much as the Britons would pay in taxes. Besides, there would be some danger in using force. "

5. Add to your list any new facts that Sources 5–8 tell you about Britain.

Activity

Now decide whether it is a good idea to invade Britain. Get into pairs.

1. On a scale of one to five indicate whether a successful invasion might be good or bad for:

	Bad				Good
■ trade	1	2	3	4	5
■ security of the border	1	2	3	4	5
■ making you more popular	1	2	3	4	5

2. How likely are you to win? Very likely? Don't know? Very unlikely?
3. What's your decision? Will you invade?
4. Now, on your own, write a speech explaining your decision. Say which of the reasons was most important in influencing you for or against an invasion.

Life in the provinces

CLAUDIUS did invade Britain. In AD43 he organised a successful campaign. There was hardly any resistance from the British, who were caught off guard. Claudius arrived for the last sixteen days, to receive the surrender of eleven English kings. He was given an immediate 'triumph' in Rome — a special procession to honour a successful military leader. A triumphal arch was built in Rome to honour him. A special coin was made, which would spread the news of the new province all around the Empire. Claudius' son was renamed Brittanicus.

So Britain became just another Roman PROVINCE. In this section we will be finding out about life in the Roman provinces, including Britain.

Look at Sources 1–4. They all show life in various Roman provinces at roughly the same period. Try to match up each picture with the correct caption from the box opposite.

▲ SOURCE 1

◄ SOURCE 2

▲ SOURCE 3

▲ SOURCE 4

Captions

Artist's reconstruction of a village in the province of Gaul

Labourers at work on a farm in Germany. From a wall painting made in the third century

A reconstructed farmhouse in southern Britain

Scenes on a farm in North Africa, from a third-century mosaic

In northern parts of the Empire, such as Britain, most farms were smallholdings, farmed by individual families. The families sometimes lived by themselves and sometimes in villages.

In other parts of the Empire, such as North Africa or Spain, there were large estates producing grapes, wine and olive oil, a lot of which was exported to Rome.

Some of these estates were divided into two parts. One part was farmed by the owner, using slaves or paid labourers. The rest was divided into small plots which were rented to tenants. They had to pay one third of their produce as rent and work on the owner's land for six days a year.

Look again at Sources 1–4.
1. What is each farmhouse made of?
2. Which ones do you think are owned by estate owners and which by peasant farmers?
3. What jobs can you see being done in Source 2?
4. Are any of these jobs mentioned in the calendar in Source 5?
5. For which part of the Roman Empire do you think this calendar was made: Britain, Spain or Germany? Explain your answer. You might find it helpful to refer to Source 2 on page 28.
6. Do you agree or disagree with this statement?
   ■ 'Farming was much the same all over the Empire.'
   Explain why.

SOURCE 5 An agricultural calendar

December Tend vines. Sow beans. Cut wood. Gather and sell olives

November Sow wheat and barley. Dig trenches to plant trees

January Sharpen stakes. Cut willows and reeds

October Harvest grapes

February Weed fields. Tend vines. Burn reeds

September Smear wine casks with pitch. Gather fruit

March Prop up and prune vines. Sow three-month wheat

August Prepare stakes. Harvest wheat. Burn stubble

April Count sheep

May Clear weeds from grain fields. Shear sheep. Wash wool. Teach oxen to pull carts. Cut animal fodder

July Harvest barley and beans

June Mow hay. Tend vines

Lullingstone villa – a study in change

At Lullingstone, on the banks of the River Darent in Kent, ARCHAEOLOGISTS have found the remains of a Roman VILLA. The buildings have been completely excavated and the evidence tells us a lot about how the building and the people living there changed over 350 years.

Stage 1: Up to AD80

Archaeologists have found the remains of a CELTIC farm. There was not enough evidence to reconstruct what it looked like, but it was probably similar to the one shown in Source 4 on the previous page.

Stage 2: AD80–280

In about AD80 a new square house called a villa was built, made of flint and mortar. It was carefully constructed and was much larger than a Celtic farmhouse. This was a new style of building in Britain, but was popular all over the Roman Empire.

- There was a large storeroom under the ground.
- The house measured twenty by fifteen metres.
- It had five rooms, with a corridor running the length of the house and a small entrance porch to one side.

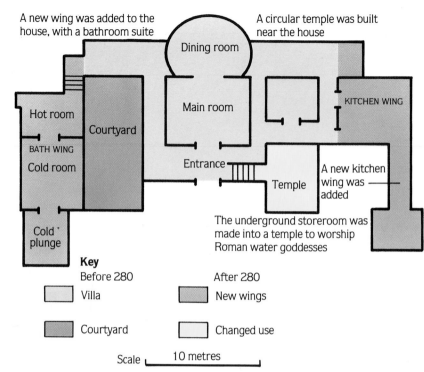

SOURCE 6 Plan of the ground floor of the villa in AD280 (Stage 3)

1. Look at Source 4 on page 32. What are the main differences between the Celtic farmhouse and the villa described in Stage 2?
2. Why have archaeologists found many more remains of the villa than of the Celtic farmhouse?

Stage 3: AD280–300

In AD280 the farmhouse was extended and improved at great expense (see Source 6). Yet it was lived in for only twenty years.

Various objects dating from this period have been found on the site, including an expensive gold ring and a statue (probably of one of the owner's ancestors) carved from Greek marble by Roman artists.

3. What evidence is there that the owner of the villa during Stage 3 was rich?
4. What evidence is there about the religious beliefs of the owner?
5. Does the villa seem to be being used in a different way than it was in Stage 2?

Stage 4: AD300–360

From AD300 the villa fell into disrepair for several years. For part of this time it was used as a small factory for TANNING leather. Then in AD330 a new series of repairs and extensions began.

The improvements included:

- a new dining room
- expensive new MOSAIC floors laid in the dining room and the living room showing the Romans' favourite gods
- a large granary built near to the house.
  Source 7 shows the villa during this period.

6. What sort of person do you think the new owner is?

SOURCE 9 From a modern book about life in Roman Britain

Large parts of the Empire were in decline in the fourth century. However, this was Britain's most prosperous period. For the first time wealthy villas became common everywhere, except in the north and west.

▲ **SOURCE 7** A reconstruction of the house in about AD360

SOURCE 8 One of the mosaic floors

8. What evidence is there of changes in religious beliefs by the owners during the five stages?
9. At which stage would you rather have lived in the villa?
10. Read Source 9. Does the evidence from Lullingstone:
   ■ support the view in Source 9 *or*
   ■ disagree with this view *or*
   ■ not help in deciding if this view is accurate?

7. Look at Source 8. Can you think of any reasons why mosaics would be an expensive way to cover the floor?

Stage 5: AD360–430

In AD370, just ten years after the Stage 4 improvements were made, one room in the house was changed into a Christian chapel. No other changes were made. Even after the house fell into disrepair again, the chapel remained in use until the fifth century, when the villa burnt down.

Activity

You have just got a job helping the information officer at Lullingstone. You have been asked to produce a short information sheet for school parties visiting the villa. It should include:
■ a title for each stage
■ a three-line description of the main changes that took place at each stage (use drawings to help you if you wish).

To make the information sheet more interesting, add your ideas about why the changes happened, and who lived there at each stage. Use the evidence to explain and support your ideas.

Use the completed information sheets to make a wall display.

How did the Romans control the Empire?

BY AD100 the Roman Empire stretched almost 3000 miles, from Scotland to the Middle East. It had a population of about 50 million people from many different races, who spoke many different languages and all worshipped their own gods.

In this section we explore how the Romans controlled this massive Empire. Did they do it by force and repression, or by treating the people well?

Organising the Empire

As we saw on page 32, the Romans divided their Empire into PROVINCES. Most provinces were controlled by a GOVERNOR, who made regular inspections of his province and held courts of law. He had a staff of 30–40 officials to help him. They included lawyers, clerks and tax collectors.

Each province paid taxes to Rome. These had to pay for the running of the province and leave Rome with a profit. Taxes were often paid in goods such as grain.

Good communications between Rome and the provinces were essential. They were provided by sea routes and the roads the Romans built. In Britain alone, 6500 miles of road were built in 100 years.

Such an efficient road system meant that the Roman army could travel very quickly to a trouble spot, or to put down a rebellion. When Julius Caesar was leading his Roman army to conquer Gaul, he travelled 800 miles in just eight days.

The army

Let's look at how the army helped Rome to keep control of its Empire.

1. Look at Source 1 carefully. Can you see the following features?
   - German prisoners of war
   - soldiers mounted on horses
   - prisoners being forced to behead their own countrymen.

   Draw the scene and label all of these things.

▼ **SOURCE 1** A scene from Marcus Aurelius' column. The column was built to honour Marcus Aurelius' successful campaign against tribes in Germany

The legions

The army was organised into legions. There were about 30 in the whole Empire. Each legion was made up of 60 centuries, each with 80 men called legionaries. Centurions were in charge of the centuries. Each legion also had 120 cavalry. There were 150,000 legionaries in total.

The soldiers in the legions served for sixteen years. They had to be Roman citizens, and most of them were volunteers. More and more, recruits came from the provinces where the legions were serving. Many were the sons of ex-soldiers who had settled there. For all these reasons, men became very proud of their legion.

The *auxilia*

These army units were made up of conquered armies and friendly tribes. The soldiers served for 25 years. They were not Roman citizens, but received citizenship at the end of their service. Many were volunteers, recruited in the province where the unit was stationed. Their armour and weapons were similar to the legionaries', but of inferior quality. Altogether, there were about 227,000 *auxilia* in the Empire, including some cavalry.

Tactics

The Romans' tactics were not very complicated. The Romans depended on their better training and discipline to win battles.

The foot-soldiers, with their shields, formed a solid barrier in the centre. Archers standing behind them fired a hail of arrows over their heads at the enemy. The cavalry fought on the flanks and were especially used for cutting down the enemy once they were retreating.

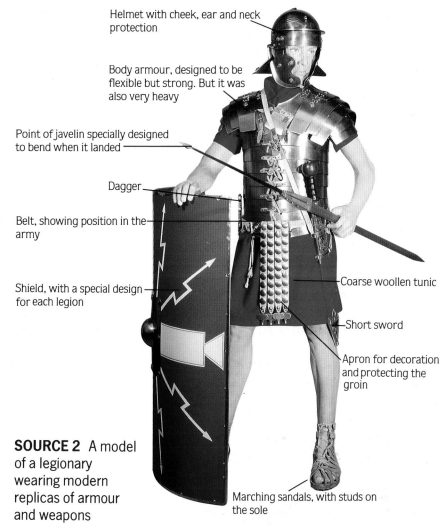

Helmet with cheek, ear and neck protection

Body armour, designed to be flexible but strong. But it was also very heavy

Point of javelin specially designed to bend when it landed

Dagger

Belt, showing position in the army

Shield, with a special design for each legion

Coarse woollen tunic

Short sword

Apron for decoration and protecting the groin

Marching sandals, with studs on the sole

SOURCE 2 A model of a legionary wearing modern replicas of armour and weapons

2. Choose three items of the legionary's equipment from Source 2 and explain how they would be useful in a battle.
3. The beginnings and endings of the following sentences have been mixed up. Using the information on these two pages, match the correct heads and tails. There are two tails for each head. Write the complete sentences in your book.

Heads	Tails
Legionaries	ran a province
	became Roman citizens when they finished their army service
Auxiliaries	collected taxes and held law courts
	served for 16 years
The governor	had to be Roman citizens
	served for 25 years

HOW DID THE ROMANS CONTROL THE EMPIRE?

Rebellion!

As you can see from Source 1 on the previous page, the Roman army could be very cruel in dealing with enemies. For example, in the province of Dacia (modern Romania), the Romans forced 100,000 local people to move right out of the province into another country. They replaced them with a completely new population from the province of Dalmatia, 400 miles away, who were more friendly to the Romans. Even so, the Romans were not always successful in keeping the peace, as the following case study from Britain shows.

In AD61 Britain had been a Roman province for less than twenty years. The Romans had not yet conquered even half of Britain (see Source 5). What's more, the estimate that Britain could be controlled by just one LEGION of the Roman army was proving to be a bad miscalculation. Four legions had been stationed in Britain since the invasion and had been kept fairly busy.

In AD61, Suetonius, the GOVERNOR of Britain, decided to conquer the Isle of Anglesey, just off Wales. Many rebellious Britons, led by the DRUID priests, were hiding there. Suetonius took two legions with him. This left the south of England almost bare of Roman troops.

While he was away, the Britons' anger against the Romans bubbled up into a full-scale rebellion.

SOURCE 3 The Roman historian Tacitus describes why the Iceni tribe rebelled

❝The King of the Iceni tribe had left his huge treasure in equal shares to his two daughters and the Emperor. But Roman tax collectors looted his lands, whipped his wife Boudicca and assaulted her two daughters. Leading members of the Iceni tribe lost their homes and lands. The relatives of the King were made slaves.❞

---

1. According to Sources 3 and 4 what caused the rebellion?
2. Are there some causes which had been building up for longer than others? Explain your answer.

▶ **SOURCE 5** The tribal areas of Britain

SOURCE 4 Tacitus describes why the Iceni's neighbours, the Trinovantes, joined the rebellion

❝What chiefly made the Trinovantes angry was how the Roman veterans had behaved when they founded the colony at Colchester. They treated the Britons cruelly. They drove them from their homes and called them slaves.

Another cause of anger was the temple built in honour of Emperor Claudius. To the British it was a symbol of everlasting slavery. The Roman priests made the Britons pay heavy taxes to use the temple.❞

The Britons defeated the Romans' Ninth Legion. Then they attacked Colchester and completely destroyed it. Archaeologists have found a layer of black soot, blackened pottery and melted glass across the whole area, dating from AD61. Every man, woman and child was massacred. The rebels went on and did the same in London and St Albans.

When Suetonius got word of this, he sent orders for the Second Legion to come from Gloucester to support him. He quickly set off back from Wales.

But the Second Legion failed to respond and suddenly Suetonius found himself face to face with a much larger force of Britons. Who would win?

Boudicca, the Queen of the Iceni, thought she would win.

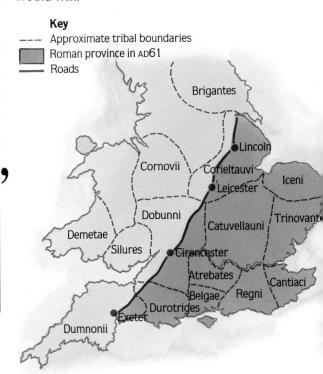

Key
- - - Approximate tribal boundaries
▭ Roman province in AD61
— Roads

Brigantes
Lincoln
Cornovii
Corieltauvi
Leicester
Iceni
Dobunni
Demetae
Silures
Catuvellauni
Trinovantes
Cirencester
Atrebates
Cantiaci
Belgae
Regni
Durotriges
Exeter
Dumnonii

SOURCE 6 In his account of the rebellion, the Roman historian Tacitus wrote down the sort of things that he thought Boudicca would have said

'The Romans will never face the din and roar of all our thousands. There are more of us and we are braver.

If we ever choose to retreat, we hide in the swamps and mountains. They cannot chase anybody or run away, because of their heavy armour.

They need bread and wine and oil, if they cannot get these, they cannot survive.'

SOURCE 8 A statue of Boudicca on her chariot, made in 1902

---

3. Look at Source 6. Why did Boudicca think she would win? Do you agree with her?
4. Look at Source 8. What impression does this give you of Boudicca?
5. This statue stands outside the Houses of Parliament in London. Does this mean that people in Britain are ashamed or proud of Boudicca?

SOURCE 9 From Tacitus' account of the rebellion

Suetonius' army was about 10,000 men strong. He chose a spot circled by woods. It had a narrow entrance and dense trees behind it. So he had no fear of an ambush. The enemy had to come at him from the front, across an open plain. He drew up his soldiers in order. The legions were in the centre. The auxiliaries were kept at the back for when they were needed. The cavalry were at the sides.

A huge number of Britons came to the battle field. They did not draw up in organised lines. Separate bands rushed up and down shouting. So sure were they of winning that they put their wives in carts on the edge of the plain.

The battle began. The narrow passage into the clearing slowed down the enemy attack. Then the Romans rushed forward in a wedge. The auxiliaries followed. The cavalry charged the enemy. The Britons fled, but got tangled up in their wagons at the rear. A dreadful slaughter followed. Neither men nor women were spared. Some writers say about 80,000 Britons were killed. The Romans lost about 4000 men. Boudicca took poison before she could be captured.

Key

✕ Possible site of battle

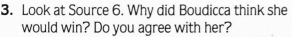

SOURCE 7 Movements of the rebels and the Roman army

---

6. Draw a plan of the battle site, showing the woods and the armies drawn up for battle.
7. Draw a plan of the battle scene, showing the movements of the armies.
8. Why did the Romans win?

There is evidence of a change of policy in Britain after Boudicca's rebellion was put down. A new governor, called Agricola, was sent to Britain. Source 10 tells you how he governed Britain.

> **SOURCE 10** A description of Agricola, governor of Britain after Boudicca's rebellion, by Tacitus
>
> 66 *He had learned from what had happened to others that an army can do little if the government is unfair. For government jobs he chose men he knew would not be greedy. He made the corn tax less heavy.*
>
> *He tried to get them to live in peace. He gave them help to build temples, public squares and good houses. He gave the sons of chiefs a Roman education. As a result the Britons were eager to speak Latin and everywhere you could see the toga [the Roman national dress] being worn. Gradually, the natives were tempted by shops, baths and rich banquets.* 99

Sources 3, 4, 6, 9 and 10 were all written by Tacitus, a Roman historian. He was the son-in-law of Agricola, and was writing at a time when Agricola's reputation was suffering in Rome. He had not seen the events he described, nor visited Britain.

However, Agricola had been a young soldier in Suetonius' army at the time of Boudicca's rebellion. There are no other accounts of the rebellion.

1. From what you now know about Tacitus say:
a) where you think he may have got his information about the rebellion from
b) whether you think his evidence will be reliable?
2. Can you think of any events in Sources 7–10 that Agricola could have seen for himself?
3. Do you think Source 10 is a reliable account of what Agricola actually did?
4. You are Agricola. Pick three of your actions from Source 10 and explain why you think they will help control the province and prevent any more rebellions.

Why did the Romans build towns?

In the eastern parts of the Empire great towns existed before the Romans came. Many of these towns were left to govern themselves and the local way of life was left untouched. But in the Western Empire towns were almost unknown before the Romans arrived.

When they conquered a new province, such as Gaul or Britain, the Romans set up three kinds of towns:

■ The most important were called colonies. Ex-soldiers were given free land in the colonies when they retired from the army.

1. Why do you think the Romans wanted their ex-soldiers to settle down in the new colonies?
2. Look back at Source 4 on page 38. What did the British most hate about the colony of Colchester?

■ Slightly less important than the colonies were the towns called *municipia*. Only Roman citizens could live in these towns, and they governed themselves. Their buildings and government were supposed to be like Rome's and were meant to show the local TRIBES the great advantages that came with Roman rule.

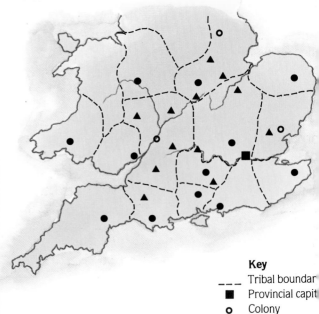

Key
_ _ _ Tribal boundary
■ Provincial capital
o Colony
● *Civitas*
▲ *Municipium*

SOURCE 11 Towns built by the Romans in Britain

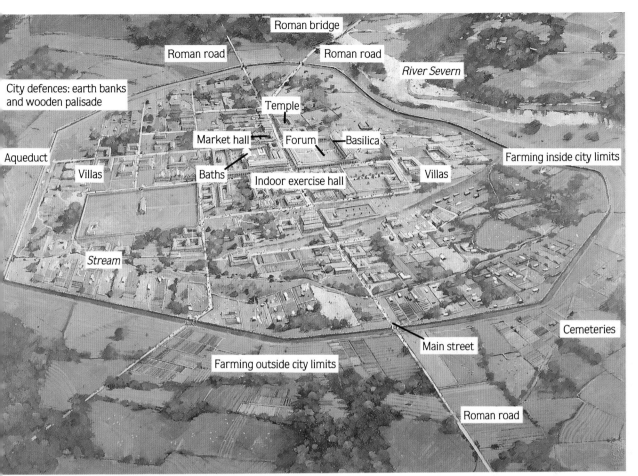

Roman bridge

Roman road

Roman road

River Severn

City defences: earth banks and wooden palisade

Temple

Market hall — Forum — Basilica

Aqueduct

Farming inside city limits

Villas

Baths

Indoor exercise hall

Villas

Stream

Cemeteries

Main street

Farming outside city limits

Roman road

SOURCE 12 Reconstruction drawing of Wroxeter, a Roman *civitas* in Britain as it was in AD150

In each tribal area the Romans set up a town called a *civitas*. This was controlled directly by the GOVERNOR of the province, but he allowed friendly tribes to play a part in governing themselves. The towns were named after the local tribe.

Wroxeter was originally the site of an important Roman fort, from AD48–90. The Romans used it as a base for their conquest of North Wales. Once Wales had been conquered, they literally packed up the fort and moved to Chester. The Wroxeter site was then used as the base for a brand new *civitas* for the Cornovii tribe. Its Roman name was Viroconium Cornoviorum. Source 12 shows the town as it was after the main public buildings were completed around AD150.

3. Look back at pages 16–21, which describe a merchant's visit to Rome. Wroxeter was the merchant's home town. Use Source 12 to draw up lists of the differences and the similarities he would have noticed between Rome and Wroxeter.

Activity

Work in pairs. One of you is a British chieftain who supports the Romans. You are trying to persuade another chief to do the same. How can you convince the other chief of the advantages of Roman rule and the dangers in opposing it?

The other chief is determined not to accept the Romans. How are you going to convince your partner that he/she is wrong to support the Romans?

Before you start, make a list of three arguments in your favour. Support them with evidence from pages 36–41.

The frontier

BRITAIN was one of the last provinces the Romans conquered. In the early days of the Empire, they did not pay much attention to defending their new provinces from attack. Rome must have seemed so strong that defence was not needed.

In the second century, however, the Emperor Hadrian was having second thoughts about the Roman frontiers. Hadrian believed the Empire should not keep trying to expand. Instead, he wanted to establish fixed frontiers that could be defended.

Activity

You are an adviser to Hadrian. Source 1 shows you the extent of the Empire in AD120. Prepare a short report to Hadrian on where new defences may be needed, and where he should consider changing the boundaries of the Empire. In particular, what should he do about the areas of the frontier where there are problems (marked A, B, C and D on Source 1)?

Mention the following in your report:
■ which parts of the Empire have strong natural boundaries such as mountains, deserts, seas or wide rivers, which make them easy to defend
■ which parts of the Empire are threatened by strong or warlike neighbours, and how you would strengthen the frontier against them
■ where you would withdraw from some occupied land to make the frontier easier to defend, or where you would expand by conquering troublesome tribes
■ how this helps with the problem of the frontiers at A, B, C and D.
    Your teacher will tell you whether you reached the same conclusions as Hadrian.

SOURCE 1 The Empire in AD120

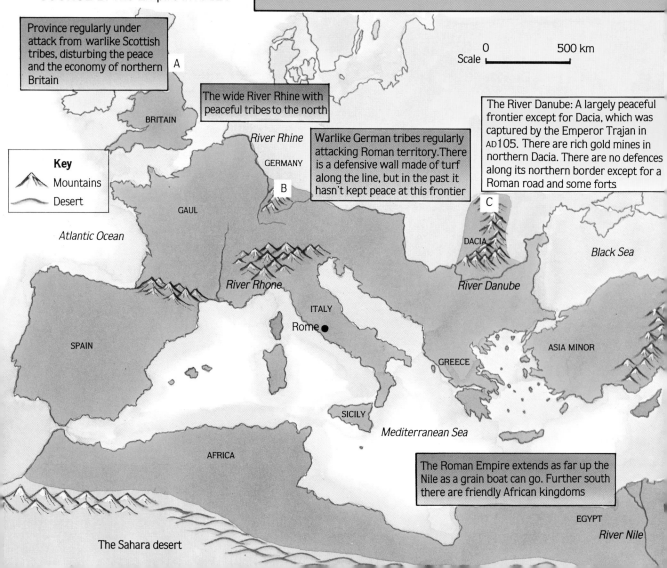

Province regularly under attack from warlike Scottish tribes, disturbing the peace and the economy of northern Britain — A

The wide River Rhine with peaceful tribes to the north

The River Danube: A largely peaceful frontier except for Dacia, which was captured by the Emperor Trajan in AD105. There are rich gold mines in northern Dacia. There are no defences along its northern border except for a Roman road and some forts

Warlike German tribes regularly attacking Roman territory. There is a defensive wall made of turf along the line, but in the past it hasn't kept peace at this frontier — B

Key
⋀ Mountains
⌒ Desert

BRITAIN

River Rhine

GERMANY

GAUL

Atlantic Ocean

River Rhone

DACIA

C

River Danube

Black Sea

ITALY

Rome ●

SPAIN

GREECE

ASIA MINOR

SICILY

Mediterranean Sea

AFRICA

The Roman Empire extends as far up the Nile as a grain boat can go. Further south there are friendly African kingdoms

EGYPT

River Nile

The Sahara desert

0   500 km
Scale

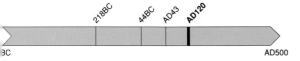
The Wall

One of the most famous frontiers is Hadrian's Wall, built in the north of Britain in AD120. Like all the Romans' frontier defences, it served various purposes:

- to show the people of the Empire that the frontier was now fixed, and fixed at a sensible point that the Romans would be able to defend
- to keep out hostile tribes and to separate the friendly tribes on the Roman side of the frontier from the hostile ones on the other side
- to help a Roman way of life to settle in: the Wall would allow people to set up towns and build villas without the constant danger of attack
- to keep the soldiers busy and disciplined, building and maintaining the Wall.

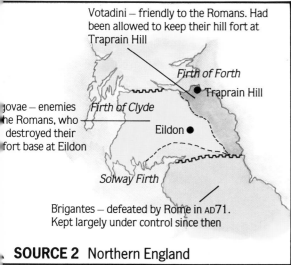

Votadini – friendly to the Romans. Had been allowed to keep their hill fort at Traprain Hill

Firth of Forth

● Traprain Hill

Firth of Clyde

...jovae – enemies ...he Romans, who destroyed their ...fort base at Eildon

Eildon ●

Solway Firth

Brigantes – defeated by Rome in AD71. Kept largely under control since then

SOURCE 2 Northern England

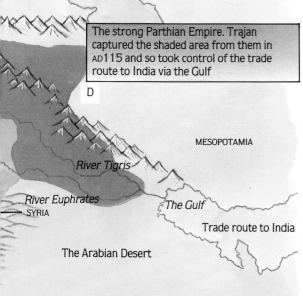

The strong Parthian Empire. Trajan captured the shaded area from them in AD115 and so took control of the trade route to India via the Gulf

D

MESOPOTAMIA

River Tigris

River Euphrates

SYRIA

The Gulf

Trade route to India

The Arabian Desert

...ea

1. Look at Source 2. You have been given the job of deciding where the wall should be. Two possible lines are shown.

    You must take into account the four points on the left. Which line will you take?

SOURCE 3 Hadrian's Wall

How successful was the Wall?

SOURCE 4 Findings from aerial surveys of archaeological sites on both sides of the Wall

❝
- There are three times as many settlements south of the Wall as north of the Wall.
- There are many more rectangular sites (a typical Roman way of building) south of the Wall.
- More sites south of the Wall are surrounded by cultivated fields.
- Many more of the settlements north of the Wall are surrounded by defensive ditches.
- There were no villas, and only a few small towns, north of the Wall.
❞

1. What does Source 4 tell us about the differences between life north and south of the Wall?

2. Does Source 4 prove that the Wall was successful in

a) separating hostile tribes from friendly tribes

b) helping a Roman way of life to settle in on the Roman side of the Wall?

Life as a soldier

What was life really like for soldiers in the Roman army? Sources 5–15 give you a range of viewpoints and different pieces of evidence. From the evidence given try to find out:
- what kind of work a soldier did when he wasn't fighting
- what kind of family life a soldier could have
- what discipline was like in the army
- what complaints soldiers had about life in the army
- what rewards soldiers got for being in the army.

SOURCE 5 From army records found at Hadrian's Wall

66*April 25 In the workshops 343 men. Of these 12 making shoes, 18 building a bath-house. Other jobs: plasterers and working in the hospital.* 99

SOURCE 6 From army records found in Egypt

66*Titus Flavius Valens:*
January 15 – making papyrus
January 17 – working in the coin mint
January 18 – working in the granary. 99

SOURCE 7 The wage records of one soldier for four months

66*Pay received:*   *75 denarii*

Deductions:	
bedding	3
rations	20
boots and straps	3
Saturnalia [winter feast]	5
tent	15
uniform	–
arms and armour	–
Total deductions:	46
Into savings bank:	29

99

SOURCE 8 Advice to the emperor Valens in AD360

66*The strength of the army is sometimes reduced by military disasters and by desertions arising from boredom with camp duties.* 99

SOURCE 9 Recent excavations in Roman forts have identified the soldier's diet

66■ *The bones of the ox are most frequently found. Sheep, pork and ham were also popular. Poultry and fish also formed part of the diet.*
■ *Grain was the basic foodstuff. It was made into bread and used as the basis of soups, porridge and pasta.*
■ *Each soldier got through a third of a ton of grain each year. Every Roman fort in Britain had sufficient supplies to last a year.*
■ *Rations while on campaign took the form of hard biscuits.*
■ *Blackberries, strawberries and cherries and beans and lentils were also eaten.*
■ *Both beer and wine were drunk. There were no dining halls. The troops either ate in the open or in their barrack rooms.*
■ *While on the march, soldiers carried rations for three days, a bronze food-box, a kettle and a portable hand-mill. Each soldier baked his own bread.*

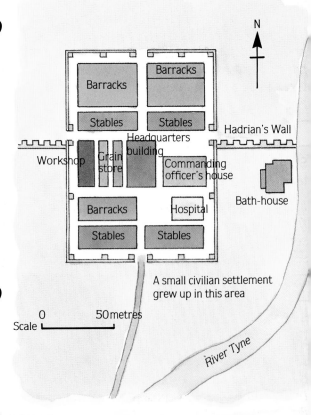

SOURCE 10 Chesters fort on Hadrian's Wall

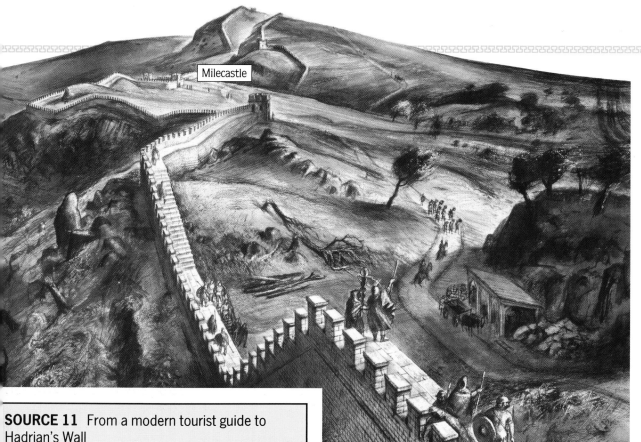

Milecastle

SOURCE 11 From a modern tourist guide to Hadrian's Wall

Every army has its camp followers. Civilian settlements grew up outside forts. As the army moved on, some of these people would move on with it. One important group in the civilian settlement would be the soldiers' wives and families. A Roman soldier was not allowed to marry, but there was nothing to stop him from having a relationship, and children, with a local woman. These 'marriages' were recognised in Roman law when the soldier retired.

SOURCE 12 Augustus decrees special privileges to military veterans in 31 BC

I have decided that all veterans shall be exempt from taxation, exempt from (further) military service and exempt from compulsory public services.

SOURCE 13 Suetonius describes Augustus' treatment of soldiers

If a company broke in battle, Augustus ordered the survivors to draw lots, then executed every tenth man and fed the remainder on barley bread instead of the usual wheat ration.

SOURCE 14 An artist's reconstruction of Roman soldiers on duty on Hadrian's Wall. The soldiers' barracks were in the milecastle

SOURCE 15 Speech by a leader of an army mutiny in the first century AD

Most of us grow old with bodies maimed with wounds. We are sent to soaking swamps and mountainous wastes. We get paid 1½ denarii a day, and out of this clothing, arms and tents have to be bought. Of floggings, and hard winters, of boring month after month, there is no end.

1. The speaker in Source 15 is trying to persuade men to join a mutiny. Do you think his account of army life can be trusted? Use the other sources to explain your answer.

Activity

Work in groups. Make a wall display about life in the Roman army. Include extracts from the evidence on this page, and add drawings or diagrams.

How civilised were the Romans?

WHAT does it mean to be civilised? It might mean any of the following to us today:

- to be clean
- to be tolerant of people who have different views
- to be advanced in science
- to like good art and literature
- to treat people well
- to value all life.

You might want to add to this list.

The Romans regarded themselves as civilised, but do you think that they really were? And did being civilised mean something different to them than it does to us today?

Let's look at some of the achievements that the Romans were most proud of.

- Their system of law. Throughout the Empire they organised courts to try to give people a fair trial.
- Their literature. In the first century BC and first century AD there was an explosion of literary activity in Italy. Poets, historians and philosophers became celebrities.
- The Romans made many new discoveries in medicine and surgery. One of the most famous doctors in the history of medicine was Galen. He was born a Greek, learned his surgery skills in a gladiator school in Roman Egypt, and then came to work in Rome itself.

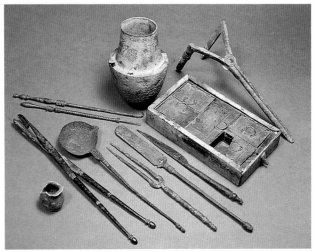

SOURCE 1 Roman surgical and midwifery instruments

1. What do you think each of the instruments in Source 1 is used for?
2. Why might a gladiator school be a good place to learn surgery?

- The Romans were also very proud of their achievements in technology. They were very clever at making things. They applied all branches of math and science to solving difficult practical problems: supplying water to cities, grinding corn more efficiently, or putting up buildings that were bigger and grander than anyone had built before.

SOURCE 2 An aqueduct in Segovia, Spain, built in the second century AD. The water is carried along the top level

Keeping clean

Now let's look at one particular area of Roman achievement – water supply and hygiene. We have already seen (on page 18) how Augustus repaired the Roman water supply. All around the Mediterranean, Roman engineers built impressive waterworks to deliver fresh water to the cities and towns of the Empire.

SOURCE 3 Written by Frontinus, Water Commissioner for Rome in AD97. His aqueducts brought in about 1000 million litres of water a day

66 *My job concerns the health of the city, and so this task has always been handled by the most important men in the state. Now nine aqueducts bring water into the city.*

The new Anio aqueduct is taken from a river which is muddy. A special filter tank was placed at the beginning of the aqueduct, where the soil could settle and the water clarify before going along the channel.

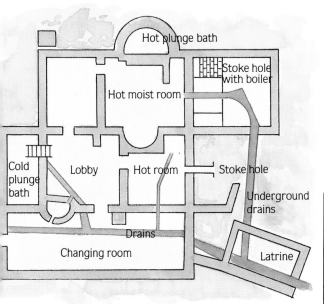

▲ **SOURCE 4** A plan of the bath-house at the Roman fort of Vindolanda

SOURCE 6 Written by Strabo, a Greek who visited Rome in the first century

Water is brought into the city through aqueducts in such quantities that it is like a river flowing through the city. Almost every house has cisterns and water pipes and fountains 〞

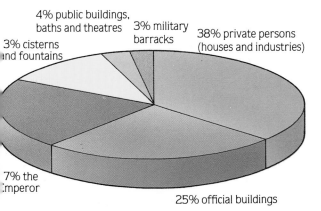

- 4% public buildings, baths and theatres
- 3% military barracks
- 3% cisterns and fountains
- 38% private persons (houses and industries)
- 7% the Emperor
- 25% official buildings

SOURCE 7 Figures for the distribution of the water supply in Rome in the first century AD

1. What evidence is there of the importance the Romans placed on clean water?
2. Do you think the water was shared out fairly?
3. Refer back to the information on page 22. Does this agree with Source 6? Explain your answer.

▶ **SOURCE 5**
How the baths were heated

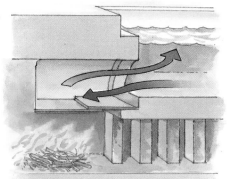

Activity

One other feature of Roman life that is important in deciding how civilised the Romans were is their art and architecture. You have seen examples of both in this unit. Now we'll look at some in more detail.

Choose one of the following two tasks. Work in groups.

1. Art

You have been asked to select pieces of art for an exhibition of the best of Roman art.

With your group, look through the whole of this unit and pick out at least three items that you would like to display in your Roman art exhibition.

You could choose from:

- the sculptures on pages 6, 25 and 36
- the MOSAICS on pages 19, 35 and 56
- the paintings on pages 2, 24 and 29
- the metalwork on the cover or on page 4.

Once you have chosen your three items, make a catalogue for your exhibition. Write a short paragraph for each item, describing what it's made of, when it was made (if you can find that out), and any special features, and explaining why you have chosen it.

Compare your choice with the choices other groups have made.

2. Architecture

Choose one of the following buildings: The Colosseum (page 50), the Roman Forum (page 21), the Circus Maximus (page 20), or Lullingstone Roman Villa (page 35).

Make a big outline drawing of the building, and stick labels to it to show its features. For example, say what materials it is made of, how big it is, what it was used for, how it is decorated, and the problems the Romans had to overcome to build it.

Slaves

The Romans took slavery for granted. For them a country without slaves was uncivilised.

From the third century BC, slaves flooded into Rome. Most were prisoners of war. Julius Caesar's conquest of GAUL alone brought in half a million slaves in five years. They were sold in the great slave markets in Rome and in other cities.

Some slaves worked and lived in rich people's houses. Others worked in mines or on large farming estates. But they all had one thing in common. They were the property of their master. They had no rights at all.

Were all slaves treated badly? The evidence in Sources 8–17 should help you to answer this question.

> **SOURCE 8** Written by a modern historian
>
> *The worst ill-treatment of slaves was in the great barracks and concentration camps of the large ranches and plantations, and the squalor of the mines. The average age of death of these men was about 21.*

> **SOURCE 9** Columella, a Spanish landowner, gives advice to owners of slaves working on farms
>
> *In the care and clothing of the slave household you should have an eye to usefulness rather than appearance, taking care to keep the slaves protected against the wind and the rain with long-sleeved leather tunics, patchwork garments or hooded cloaks. If you do this, no weather is so unbearable that some work may not be done in the open.*

SOURCE 10 An iron collar for a slave. The writing says: 'I have run away. Catch me. If you take me back to my master Zoninus you'll be rewarded.' The collar was riveted on

SOURCE 11 A tombstone for a slave erected by his master. Part of the inscription reads, 'the most faithfu slave'

> **SOURCE 12**
> a) Written by the Roman writer Pliny to the Emperor Trajan
>
> *I find in several cities certain persons who work and are paid as public slaves or as clerks in the civil service, despite being condemned to the mines and the public games. How should I deal with them?*
>
> b) Trajan's reply
>
> *Those whose sentences have not been reversed should be sent back to their punishments, but let those who have grown old work at the public baths, cleanse the sewers or repair the streets.*

SOURCE 13 The writer Seneca writing to a friend about how slaves should be treated

I am glad to learn from those who bring news from you that you live on friendly terms with your slaves. This is right for a sensible and well educated man like yourself.
    'They are slaves,' people say. No. They are men.

SOURCE 16 From a modern history of the Roman Empire

When wars became less frequent, the supply of slaves began to dry up and they became more expensive. The Emperor Claudius stopped masters killing their slaves without good reason, and Domitian stopped the castration of slaves for commercial reasons.

SOURCE 14 A carving from a Roman tomb from AD100. A stone carving is being lifted by a crane powered by slaves walking around inside a treadmill wheel

SOURCE 17 Reconstruction of mills built in France in AD310. Together, the eight mills could grind as much corn in one hour as 800 slaves could have done previously

SOURCE 15 A Roman historian explains the causes of a slave revolt in Sicily in the first century

The Sicilians brought the slaves down in droves from the markets and immediately branded them with marks on their bodies. Oppressed by hard work and beatings, the slaves could endure it no longer.

After one revolt 6000 slaves were crucified along the Appian Way (a road leading into Rome).

1. List all the different jobs slaves did according to Sources 8–17.
2. What evidence is there that slaves were treated badly?
3. What evidence is there that slaves were treated well?
4. What evidence is there in Sources 16 and 17 that the situation of slaves changed as time went by? How did it change?
5. From the evidence, how do you think a Roman would justify owning slaves?
6. Do you think the Romans were wrong to keep slaves? Give your reasons, and refer to the evidence in Sources 8–17.

The murderous games

Source 18 shows one of the grandest buildings in Rome. Most of it is still standing today. The Romans reserved their best architecture for their most important buildings. And yet this magnificent building was created to allow people to watch gladiators fighting to the death, criminals being executed publicly and prisoners of war being mauled by wild animals.

SOURCE 19 A nineteenth-century view of Roman gladiators fighting in the Colosseum

Source 19 shows the professional fighters – the gladiators – fighting in the arena. The gladiators were mostly slaves and criminals, and had been highly trained in special gladiator schools. There were some women gladiators (see page 25). If gladiators were lucky and survived their many fights they could win their freedom.

The gladiator fights started around 260BC. The Romans believed that the souls of the dead needed human blood, and so at funerals they killed prisoners or slaves. Over the next 200 years the gladiator shows developed out of this. In 65BC, Julius Caesar held funeral games for his father where 640 gladiators fought, and criminals were forced to fight with wild beasts.

Soon the gladiator fights were held purely for enjoyment. Members of rich families paid for the games to be held and tried to make theirs the biggest and bloodiest games.

But the most spectacular shows were organised by the Emperors. Along with hand-outs of free grain, the spectacular and bloody shows were the best way of keeping the ordinary Romans on the Emperor's side. The Emperor Trajan held games in

▼ **SOURCE 18** The Colosseum in Rome – the most magnificent amphitheatre in the Roman Empire

Masts for cables which could support a giant sunshade for daytime shows or a vast chandelier for night-time shows

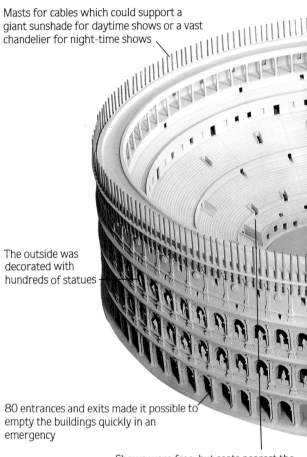

The outside was decorated with hundreds of statues

80 entrances and exits made it possible to empty the buildings quickly in an emergency

Shows were free, but seats nearest the arena were reserved for rich people

AD108 lasting 123 days, where 9138 gladiators fought and 11,000 animals were killed. On a single day 3000 men were killed.

Going to watch the fights could be dangerous. One day, when they ran out of criminals, the Emperor Caligula ordered that a whole section of the crowd should be thrown to the wild beasts.

However, not all Romans liked the games.

SOURCE 20 From a letter written by Cicero to a friend in the first century AD

❝What pleasure can it possibly be to a man of culture when either a puny human being is mangled by a powerful beast, or a splendid animal is transfixed with a hunting spear?

Seating for 50,000 people to watch men and animals fighting each other to the death

The arena floor could be made watertight and flooded for mock naval battles

The arena floor was made of sand to absorb the blood of the victims

Underneath the arena was a maze of corridors and rooms to keep the gladiators, wild animals and prisoners before they were taken up to the arena for their fight to the death. Hidden trap-doors and ingenious machines allowed fighters and animals to appear from beneath the earth

For many Romans, however, the gladiators were glamorous figures, like modern film stars. MOSAICS, statues and drawings were made showing top gladiators. At Pompeii, you can still see messages that girls scratched into the wall about their heart-throbs. Some gladiators even volunteered for the job. In Source 22 the writer Juvenal writes about a senator's wife who eloped to Egypt with her favourite fighter.

SOURCE 22

66 *What did she see in him to make her put up with being called 'The Gladiator's Moll'? He wasn't exactly young, and he had a dud arm. Besides, his face looked a proper mess, helmet-scarred, a great wart on his nose, an unpleasant discharge always trickling from one eye. But he was a gladiator. This made her prefer him to her children, her country, her sister and her husband.* 99

1. Use the information on this page to write two paragraphs about why you think the games were so popular with the ordinary Romans.
2. Is there any evidence that not all Romans liked the games?
3. Work in pairs. You have been given the opportunity to interview a) a gladiator, and b) an Emperor, about the games. What questions do you want to ask each of them? Draw up a list of questions. What answers would you expect them to give?

SOURCE 21 Written by the Roman historian Seneca

I arrived at the Colosseum in the middle of the day. A mass execution of criminals was taking place. This was meant to be entertainment for the crowd while they waited for the gladiators.

No sooner has a man killed his rival than the crowd shout for him to kill another, or be killed. In the end every fighter dies. And all this with half the seats still empty.

You may object that the victims are murderers and thieves, but even if they deserve to suffer, why watch their sufferings? 99

1. Use Sources 1, 3, 13 and 20 to describe how civilised the Romans were.
2. If you use Sources 8, 9, 18 and 21 to describe how civilised the Romans were, how does your view change?

Ｈow tolerant were the Romans?

YOU may think that one important part of being civilised is to be tolerant of other people's beliefs. We are now going to investigate whether the Romans were tolerant or not.

The Romans governed many different races, who worshipped many different gods. How tolerant were the Romans of the different religious beliefs of the people they conquered?

SOURCE 1 Written by Polybius, a Greek visitor to Rome in the second century AD

❝ *What keeps the Empire united is religion. It is cloaked in so much pomp, and plays such a large part in private and public affairs, that nothing can fight its influence. The government encourages it for the sake of the common people, whose lawless desires and violent anger are kept under control by invisible terrors and great ceremonies.* ❞

---

1. What does Polybius tell us about the general attitude of the Roman government towards religion?
2. Is he stating facts or opinions? Explain your answer.

Roman religion would not be regarded as a religion by many people today. It did not involve any emotional or spiritual commitment. The Romans' approach was a practical one. They carried out the right actions, and in return the gods gave them a more comfortable and successful life.

People prayed and made offerings at temples to ask for help or to thank the gods for a favour.

There were few full-time PRIESTS. Most priests were important officials in the government, for whom being a priest was just one of several jobs. The Emperor was the chief priest. From the first century AD on, emperors were worshipped as gods after they died.

People also worshipped at home. They had household gods, who were seen as the guardians of the house. Houses had a SHRINE called the *lararium* where family ceremonies took place (see Source 2).

As the Romans conquered new territories, they came across new gods and goddesses. Let's look at three examples and see how the Romans dealt with them.

SOURCE 2 A *lararium*

Britain: Sulis

The Britons worshipped many of their own gods. At the hot springs at Bath they worshipped a goddess called Sulis. When the Romans built a town there and developed the baths they called the town Aquae Sulis (Waters of Sulis) and built a temple to the goddess. They combined the worship of Sulis with worship of their own goddess Minerva.

Persia: Mithras

Mithras was a Persian god concerned with the struggle between good and evil. The religion had many secret rituals and practices. It was a favourite religion of many Roman soldiers. The religion was for men only.

Greece: Asclepios

Asclepios was a Greek god who was adopted by the Romans. They built temples to him in Rome. They believed that if you were ill and slept at Asclepios' temple the god would cure you during the night.

---

1. According to these examples, how did the Romans deal with the gods and goddesses of people they conquered?
2. Why do you think they had this policy?

One important thing about all of these foreign gods, as far as the Romans were concerned, was that they could be worshipped alongside Roman gods. In fact, Roman gods had a lot in common with them. As long as their priests did not tell people to reject Roman rule, and as long as the people in the provinces continued to worship the Emperor and did not cause trouble, the Romans did not mind which gods they followed.

However, we are now going to look at three other case studies, which show that the Romans had a different attitude to religions which brought their followers into conflict with the rules or the needs of the Empire.

Case study 1: the Druids

The DRUIDS were priests in GAUL and Britain. They claimed they were the only people who knew the secrets of the gods. They were respected by the leaders of the TRIBES. They were often asked for advice. They understood the cycles of the seasons and had made calendars, showing which months were good for certain activities.

The Romans were determined to wipe out the Druids. They chased them all the way to their stronghold on the island of Anglesey, off the Welsh coast, and killed all of them. Why did the Romans treat the Druids this way? Sources 3 and 4 suggest one reason.

SOURCE 4 A picture of a Druid human sacrifice, drawn in 1676. It was based on a description written by Julius Caesar after his invasion of Britain in 54BC (although he almost certainly didn't see a sacrifice)

SOURCE 3 Written by the Roman historian Tacitus

The Druids covered their altars with the blood of their prisoners and the ripped-out guts of men sacrificed to their gods.

After conquering Anglesey [in AD61], Suetonius' men hacked down the religious woods, dedicated to devil worship and foul ceremonies.

Tacitus also offers us some other information (see Source 5):

SOURCE 5

■ *Anglesey was a popular hiding place for rebellious Britons.*
■ *When the Britons fought, the Druids stood in ranks, their hands uplifted, calling to the gods for help.*

1. When Suetonius attacked Anglesey it was only about 200 years since the Romans had stopped human sacrifices in their own religion. What do you think Romans would feel about a religion that still included human sacrifice? Do you think this would explain their dislike of the Druids?

2. Do the two statements in Source 5 suggest reasons why the Romans finished off the Druids? Explain your answer.

HOW TOLERANT WERE THE ROMANS?

At the other end of the Empire the Romans found themselves facing problems with two other religious groups, the Jews and the Christians.

Case study 2: the Jews

The home of the Jewish religion was the tiny kingdom of Judaea. Source 6 shows that this area was vital to Rome for many reasons.

Unlike Britain, Judaea was not a Roman province. But it was dominated by Rome. From time to time parts of Judaea were absorbed into the Roman province of Syria. At other times Rome appointed a governor to run Judaea. But as long as it was peaceful the Romans saw no need officially to make it a province.

Until 4BC Judaea was ruled by a strong King, Herod the Great. He was a keen supporter of the Romans and a friend of the Roman Emperor Augustus. At this time the Romans treated the Jews well. For example:
■ The Jews were excused service in the Roman army because it would involve them breaking some of their religious rules.

■ The Romans turned a blind eye to features of the Jewish religion that they disagreed with — for example the idea that there was only one God.
■ The Roman Emperor Augustus — who was not a Jew — paid for daily sacrifices in the Jews' Temple in Jerusalem.

Early in the first century AD most Jewish leaders were pro-Roman. When one of the kings of Judaea started breaking Jewish religious laws the Jews' leaders appealed directly to Rome for help and the King was removed.

Not all Jews lived in Judaea. There were Jewish communities in other cities in the Empire. Source 7, for example, concerns the Jews living in Rome.

> **SOURCE 7** A decree of Augustus in AD2 or 3
>
> "Since the Jewish nation has been found well disposed to the Roman people, it has been decided that the Jews may follow their own customs . . . And if anyone is caught stealing their sacred items, his property shall be confiscated.

1. From the evidence so far choose two words from the following list which best describe the attitude of the Romans to the Jewish religion, Then write four sentences explaining why you have chosen these two words.
   - critical
   - friendly
   - supporting
   - angry
   - tolerant
   - intolerant

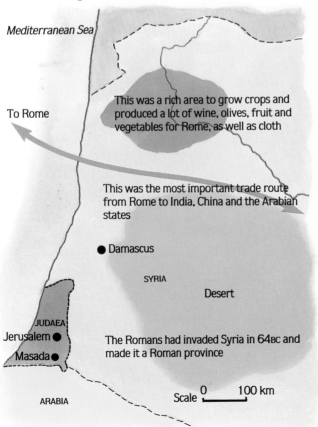

Mediterranean Sea

To Rome

This was a rich area to grow crops and produced a lot of wine, olives, fruit and vegetables for Rome, as well as cloth

This was the most important trade route from Rome to India, China and the Arabian states

● Damascus

SYRIA

Desert

JUDAEA
Jerusalem ●
Masada ●

The Romans had invaded Syria in 64BC and made it a Roman province

ARABIA

Scale 0 — 100 km

SOURCE 6 Syria and Judaea in the first century AD

Over the next 60 years the situation began to change. Herod had been a strong King. But his successors were the opposite. Judaea had one political crisis after another. Some Roman officials who were sent to help sort out these problems made them worse. For example, Pontius Pilate upset the Jews by breaking their religious rules and helped to stir up disagreements between opposing groups of Jews.

By AD60 there were some Jewish groups, including many chief priests, who supported Rome. Other groups, such as the poorer priests and a group called the Zealots, were opposed to the Romans and to any Jews who supported Rome.

Things came to a head in AD66. The Zealots revolted. They drove the Roman soldiers out of Jerusalem and took control of the Temple.

The Roman Emperor sent an army of 50,000 soldiers to Judaea. They dealt harshly with the rebels. Up to one million Jews were killed. Thousands of others were transported to their deaths in AMPITHEATRES. Jerusalem was captured. The Zealots were burned alive in the Temple. And Titus, one of the Roman generals, sacrificed a pig in the Temple, which was a terrible insult to the Jews.

The revolt was crushed, but that was not the end of the Zealots' resistance. In AD73 one group took over the mountain fortress of Masada.

SOURCE 8 The Jewish historian Josephus tells the story

The new governor in Judaea was Flavius Silva. He saw that only one fortress held out against the Romans. The fortress was Masada. He built a siege wall right round the fortress, with camps so that no one could escape.

The Romans occupied a spur of rock and built a solid earth platform on top. On this they built a base of stones, and on this a tower 27 m high, protected all over with iron plates. This tower was for catapults and stone throwers. A great battering ram was brought up to the platform and swung continuously against the fortress wall until it was smashed.

Josephus records the end of the battle. First, he makes up words which the Jewish leader might have said (see Source 10).

SOURCE 10

  'It is clear that at daybreak our resistance will come to an end. But we are free to choose an honourable way to die with those we love. Let us die without becoming slaves to our enemies.'

Ten were chosen by lot to be the executioners of the rest, and everyone – men with their wives and children – lay down and offered their throats to those who had to perform the painful duty. So finally the nine presented their throats, and the one man left set fire to the palace and drove his sword through his own body and fell down beside his family.

1. Make a tracing of the outline of the fortress of Masada in Source 9. Mark on it where you think the Romans built the siege wall, the earth platform and the tower.
2. Are there any parts of Josephus' account that you think cannot be trusted?
3. Why do you think the Romans treated the Jewish rebels so harshly?
4. Why do you think the Jews at Masada killed themselves?

SOURCE 9 Photograph of Masada

Spur of rock occupied by Romans

Pathway to the fortress

Herod's palace

HOW TOLERANT WERE THE ROMANS?

Case study 3: the Christians

The Christians were followers of Jesus Christ. Christianity began life as an offshoot from the Jewish religion. In around AD30 Jewish leaders in Judaea were worried about a new PROPHET, Jesus.

> **SOURCE 11** From an account of the events written some years later
>
> 66 *Jesus was called by his followers Christ (the chosen one of God). His own people, the Jews, did not like this. They brought him to trial and handed him over to the Roman governor, Pontius Pilate, to be executed.* 99

Pilate saw no reason to crucify Jesus. But he bowed to Jewish pressure, and, because he feared a riot, he agreed to crucify Jesus. However, Jesus' followers did not give up. Not many years later the new religion of Christianity (named after Christ) was spreading around the Roman Empire, and even to Rome itself.

> **SOURCE 12** Written by the historian Tacitus about events in AD64. The city of Rome had been badly damaged by a massive fire
>
> 66 *Nero [the Roman Emperor] put the blame for the fire on the Christians. Accordingly, they were all arrested. An enormous number were convicted. Mockery of every sort was added to their deaths. They were covered with the skins of beasts, and torn apart by dogs; or were nailed to crosses; or were condemned to the flames and burnt to serve as lighting when the sun had gone down.* 99

> **1.** Look at Source 12. How has the attitude of the Romans towards the Christians changed since AD30?

Sources 13–17 will help you decide for yourself why the Romans changed their minds about the Christians.

Some of the Christian leaders began to spread Christianity well beyond Syria. They included Paul, who was a Roman citizen. He made three journeys to cities in Asia, Macedonia and Achaea to teach people about Christianity. Eventually he was arrested and taken to Rome and was probably executed in AD66.

Christians like Paul taught that there was only one God. They wouldn't make offerings to any of the Romans' gods.

> **SOURCE 13** An extract from the *Acts of the Apostles*. In Ephesus (in the Roman province of Asia Minor) a silversmith complained that Paul was ruining his business of making silver models of Roman gods
>
> 66 *Paul is telling them that gods made by human hands are not gods at all. There is danger for us here. Not only that our line of business will get a bad name, but also that the temple of Diana – the goddess who is worshipped by everyone in Asia and in all the world – will come to mean nothing.* 9

> **SOURCE 14** In the third century, Christians had to take a loyalty test. This is the sort of certificate they were given if they passed
>
> 66 *We, Aurelia Bellias, daughter of Peteres, and her daughter Capinis, have always sacrificed to the gods, and now in your presence have sacrificed and eaten the sacred offerings.* 9

56

SOURCE 15 Written by the Emperor Trajan to one of his officials

Christians should be punished unless they prove they are not Christian by worshipping our gods. 99

2. According to Sources 14 and 15, how did Christians prove they were loyal to the Emperor?
3. Not all Christians were prepared to do this. Can you think of reasons why they might not want to?

SOURCE 16 Written by a modern religious writer

The real strength of Christianity, which made it outstrip all other religions, was its message of love and hope for everybody. This love and hope was extended to women, and even the poor and those that society had rejected. 99

SOURCE 17 A mosaic showing Christians being killed by wild animals in an amphitheatre

The persecution of Christians continued for many years. They suffered many extreme punishments.

For safety, Christians in Rome started to meet in secret in underground caves. This made the government even more suspicious, because they thought the Christians were plotting against the government.

Despite this persecution, Christianity continued to spread and grow, and 250 years after St Paul's journeys to the Mediterranean, Christianity was the most popular religion in the Empire.

Now look back at Sources 13–17 and use evidence from them to answer these questions.
4. How did the Romans treat Christians?
5. Why were the Romans worried about the Christians?
6. Can you find any evidence to explain why Christianity was so popular?

Different outcomes

The Druids were wiped out. The Jews survived as a persecuted minority in the Empire. But Christianity grew, until in 337 the Emperor Constantine became a Christian and Christianity became the official religion of the Empire. By 400 the Romans were spreading Christianity into the provinces, and the traditional religions of the Empire were themselves being put down.

1. On pages 52–57 we have studied the Roman treatment of three different religious groups. Do you think the Romans were right to be worried about:
   ■ the Druids
   ■ the Jews
   ■ the Christians?
2. How could they have dealt with each group other than the way they did?

Activity

You have been asked to write a list of guidelines for government officials in first-century Rome, to help them decide whether a new religion is to be tolerated or not. Work in groups, and using any of the evidence on pages 52–57 write at least three guidelines.

Problems in the Empire

IN AD369 an anonymous writer sent a document to the Emperor Valens. Like many other people in the Empire, he was very worried about the problems facing it. In his 'treatise' he describes the problems and suggests some solutions, which are occasionally rather far-fetched.

SOURCE 1 From the introduction to the treatise

❝I shall describe:
- how taxes can be reduced by half
- how settlers can be persuaded to develop frontier lands without anxiety
- how the gold and silver you [the Emperor] own can be doubled
- how you can please the soldiers by giving them more rewards than usual.

I shall also show:
- how a particularly fast warship is able, through a brilliant invention, to defeat ten other ships and sink them, without need for a large crew
- how a new invention can allow a horse to charge the enemy lines without needing a rider on his back
- how a new type of military bridge has been invented which can be carried around by a small number of men and 50 packhorses.❞

---

1. What evidence is there in Source 1 that:
   - the government was running out of money
   - people felt they were paying too much tax
   - the army could not afford to pay as many soldiers as it needed?

The writer then goes on to explain his ideas about why things have gone wrong and various things he believes the Emperor should do:

SOURCE 2 Extracts from the treatise

❝■ Public grants have made the rich even more extravagant, while the poor are driven by their problems into crime.
■ Now, in addition, comes the appalling greed of the provincial governors, which ruins the taxpayers.
■ The vast spending on the army must be stopped.
■ Above all, it must be recognised that wild nations are pressing upon the Roman Empire and howling round about it everywhere. Treacherous barbarians, protected by natural defences, are attacking every frontier. The state must take care of the frontier.
■ When you've dealt with all these, one thing remains to you, Emperor – to get rid of dishonest laws.

The problems of the Roman Empire have been a favourite subject for historians to write about. Sources 4–6 come from three different histories of the Empire. They give us some extra information about some of the problems already mentioned, and add some new problems as well.

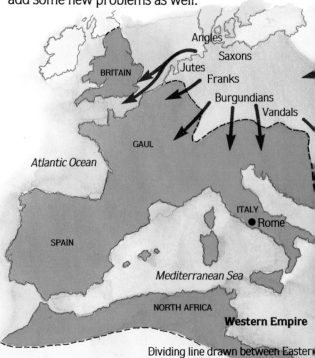

▶ **SOURCE 3** The Roman Empire and the barbarian tribes which threatened it. Since AD330 the Empire had been ruled from the Eastern capital, Constantinople

Dividing line drawn between Eastern and Western Empires in 395

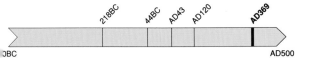
SOURCE 4

The Empire's biggest single expenditure was the army. To pay for the army taxes had risen so much that an ordinary Roman was paying up to one third of his income in taxes and another one third in rent. 99

SOURCE 5

With no fixed method of choosing the next Emperor, there was nothing to stop cruel and selfish men from fighting for power. Time after time, successful generals marched their legions into Rome and killed the reigning Emperor, only to suffer the same fate themselves. In the space of 73 years there were 23 emperors, 20 of whom were murdered. 99

SOURCE 6

By the fourth century it was becoming very clear that the defensive system set up during the second century had a major flaw. It was too much like a lobster. Once attackers got through the armoured outer shell, there was nothing inside but undefended fleshy parts.

The Roman road system, which had served the Roman army so well when they were always on the attack, had allowed invaders to push deep into the Empire as soon as they got through the walls. 99

SOURCE 7 Border security was increased all over the Empire. Even in far-away Britain in the fourth century, the Romans built a series of coastal defences called the forts of the Saxon shore. This one is Pevensey Castle in Sussex

Huns

Eastern Goths

Western Goths   Black Sea

Constantinople

ASIA MINOR

Eastern Empire

Activity

Work in pairs or groups.
1. Using all the sources on this page, make a list of problems facing the Empire.
2. Write each problem on a separate piece of paper.
3. Arrange the problems in order of importance. Put the biggest problem first. If you think two problems are equally important place them alongside each other.
4. Take the problems in order, starting from the top. In your group, try to think of solutions to that problem.
5. Sometimes your solutions to one problem might make another problem worse. Check each of your solutions against the other problems.
6. Now, on your own, write a 'Discussion paper' to be presented to the Emperor's advisers.
a) Set out the problems facing the Empire.
b) Suggest solutions that can be adopted.

PROBLEMS IN THE EMPIRE

The decline of the West

The BARBARIAN tribes first crossed the Rhine in AD406. There had been regular raids for as long as the Empire had existed, but now the worn out Roman army and its inefficient leaders couldn't resist any longer. German tribesmen poured into the Empire looking for land to settle in. In 410 they reached Rome itself, and stripped it of many of its treasures.

The government in Rome sent a famous message to the British leaders. The British had appealed for help to fight off barbarian tribes who were making regular raids on the English coast. The British got the message back, 'You must look to your own defences.' In other words, the Romans meant 'We've got enough problems of our own in Rome. Please look after your own problems yourselves.'

In 476 the last western Emperor, Romulus Augustulus, lost his power. A barbarian King, Ordovocar, took over Italy and ruled his kingdom from Rome. Throughout Western Europe the Roman influence gradually, rather than suddenly, gave way to the new influence of the barbarian tribes.

---

1. Compare Source 8 with Source 3 on the previous page. Describe the changes that have happened in 100 years.

▼ **SOURCE 8** What had happened to the Roman Empire by AD476

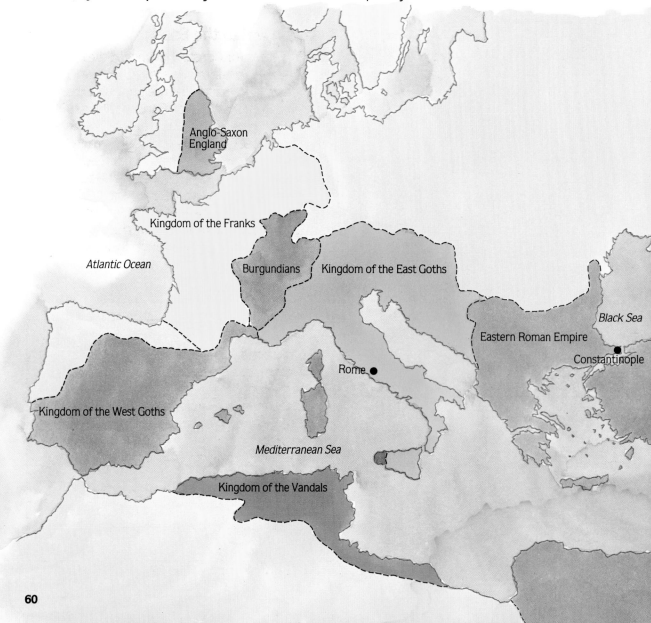

Anglo-Saxon England

Kingdom of the Franks

Atlantic Ocean

Burgundians　Kingdom of the East Goths

Black Sea

Eastern Roman Empire

Constantinople

Rome ●

Kingdom of the West Goths

Mediterranean Sea

Kingdom of the Vandals

SOURCE 9 This ivory box, showing an attack on a Roman-walled town, was made by Frankish craftsmen in the fifth century

2. Look at Source 9. Can you find:
- the Frankish attackers
- archers falling from the walls of the town
- townspeople sheltering in a church.

The survival of the East

After the Emperor Constantine moved the capital of the Empire to Constantinople in AD330, the Eastern Empire was wealthier and more populated than the West. The Pope, head of the Christian Church (now the official religion of the Empire), was in Rome, but the important affairs of the Empire were dealt with from Constantinople. And although the Eastern Empire suffered economic problems and barbarian attacks as well, it survived for a further 1000 years. Under its new name, the Byzantine Empire, it remained a powerful force around the Mediterranean until it was overrun by invaders in 1453.

1. What date would you choose as the date of the end of the Roman Empire? Here are some possibilities. You might want to add a different date altogether.
   395: when the Empire officially split in two
   410: when Rome was sacked by barbarian invaders
   476: when the last western Emperor was removed
   1453: when the Eastern Empire was destroyed.
   Take a vote in the class to see which is the favourite date.

What have the Romans given us?

Is THERE any evidence that even though the Roman Empire declined its influence continued?

Roads
- In Britain, several of our main roads – e.g. the A1 (London to Scotland) or the A5 (London to North Wales) – follow the old lines of Roman roads.

Places and place names
- Some of our most important cities were founded by the Romans, e.g. London.
- Some places take their names from their Roman name, e.g. London from *Londinium*.

Calendar
- The calendar we use today, with 365 days in a year, is based on the one developed by Julius Caesar.
- All the months of the year take their names from the Roman months.
- Some days of the week are named after Roman gods.

1. Which month is named after Julius Caesar, and which one after Mars, the god of war?
2. Which day of the week is named after Saturn, the Roman god of farmers?

Literature
- Many stories, plays, poems and histories have survived from the Roman period. Probably the most famous is the *Aeneid*, written by Virgil.

Language
- Latin is still spoken in some sections of the Roman Catholic Church. Until ten years ago all services in Roman Catholic churches were said in Latin.
- Latin has influenced the way European languages such as French, Spanish, Italian and English have developed.
- All British coins have a Latin inscription.
- We've borrowed many words from Latin to use in English, e.g. *versus, et cetera, exit*.

3. Look at a pound coin. See if you can work out where the Latin is.

Religion
- Christianity was adopted as the official religion of the Roman Empire in AD337 and remains the dominant religion in most countries which once formed a part of the Empire.

Buildings
- Some Roman buildings – e.g. the Roman baths in Bath – are still standing today, which shows how well built they were.
- Roman styles have been copied in many places at different times, e.g. public buildings such as museums, town halls and even schools built in Britain in the nineteenth century.

Health and medicine
- Roman ideas about public health, surgery and patient care were picked up by ISLAMIC doctors and later by European doctors.

Science
- In science, plants, animals, insects and even mushrooms are known officially by Latin names.

Law
- Aspects of British law – the way the courts are run, names of officials and the way cases are recorded – have all developed from Roman law.

Activity

Historians call the influence a society has on societies that come after it a legacy. What is the Roman legacy?

Work in small groups.
1. Write out each of the pieces of information on this page on a separate piece of card.
2. Sort the cards into three piles:
a) things that still play a part in your life today
b) things that don't play a part in your life today
c) things you cannot decide about.
   You may need to refer to earlier pages in the unit for more information about a subject.
3. You are going to have a class debate. Prepare a case for or against this statement: 'The Romans have no relevance for us today.' You should consider:
- whether the Roman legacy plays a part in *your* life today.
- whether the Roman legacy plays a part in *other people's* lives today.